T0244272

THE HARD ROAD WILL TAKE YOU HOME

With an impressive 13 years of distinguished and decorated military service, Anthony 'Staz' Stazicker was awarded the Conspicuous Gallantry Cross for combat actions in 2013. Staz left the UK Special Forces in 2018 and launched the technical clothing company, ThruDark. ThruDark is now known as one of the best high-performance outerwear brands in the UK.

ANTHONY 'STAZ' STAZICKER CGC

THE HARD ROAD WILL TAKE YOU HOME

WHAT THE MILITARY ELITE TEACHES US ABOUT INNOVATION, ENDEAVOUR AND NEXT LEVEL SUCCESS

Published in hardback in Great Britain in 2023 by Allen & Unwin,
an imprint of Atlantic Books Ltd.

10 9 8 7 6 5 4 3 2 1

A CIP catalogue record for this book is available from the British Library.

Hardback ISBN: 978 1 83895 733 9
E-book ISBN: 978 1 83895 734 6

Typeset by Avon DataSet Ltd, Alcester, Warwickshire

Printed and bound by CPI Group (UK) Ltd, Croydon, CR0 4YY

Allen & Unwin
An imprint of Atlantic Books Ltd
Ormond House
26–27 Boswell Street
London
WC1N 3JZ

www.atlantic-books.co.uk

MIX
Paper | Supporting
responsible forestry
FSC® C171272
FSC
www.fsc.org

Contents

FOREWORD

by Jason Fox

I first met Staz while serving abroad with the military. He'd been posted on a long deployment and I was part of the incoming group that were set to take over. During the handover period we trained a few times and worked on a couple of jobs together. As I got to see what he was all about I remember thinking, 'What a hoofing bloke,' and we became good mates. Staz was a beast. He'd put everything into his gym sessions as he would his work – in and out of the military – and it really didn't surprise me when he was later awarded the Conspicuous Gallantry Cross for Combat Actions conducted while scrapping with the UK Armed Forces.

During his military career, Staz proved how innovative thought could bring success, especially when twinned with hard-core endeavour. When he left the military to launch the massively successful technical clothing company ThruDark with our mutual friend Louis Tinsley, those skills and processes were then transferred into business. Success inevitably followed. Now all of that intel has been stuffed into the book you're about to read. If you only put 50 per cent of what you learn here into practice, I reckon you'll be on to a winner.

That's because Staz's processes have been battle-tested – *literally*. When he first launched ThruDark, I knew he was on to something because, like many former military types, he was disciplined and able to exploit both success and failure, willing to push through discomfort, and constantly in search of excellence. ThruDark was a cracking idea too.

Why? Well, I've often moaned about the type of technical gear I've been forced to use in the most hostile environments on earth, whether I was serving or during an expedition. What I didn't know was just how bloody good ThruDark would be at revolutionising the concept of outdoor kit, though that all changed when I trekked to the North Pole wearing the first official ThruDark expedition parka. It was amazing. The coat didn't fail me at any point, and if it hadn't been auctioned off for charity upon my return, I'd still be using it now.

But even though the kit was a success, ThruDark wasn't content to rest on its laurels, which is a trait of both the UK military and a top-level business. Staz and Louis wanted to make improvements. They also needed to understand what tweaks could be made to the design in a process known as the After Action Report (AAR), which was initiated by something called a hot debrief. This was just one of the many battle tactics that could be applied to all sorts of real-life scenarios – business, learning, entrepreneurship, innovation and even relationships. Don't worry, you'll read about them all here.

It's inspiring that Staz has written about the personal techniques and strategies that have elevated him to the next level, because the biggest compliment I can pay ThruDark is that they make me wish for winter. Having seen the way their business works I want to push myself harder in how I think about expeditions, new challenges and different projects. My guess is that after putting down *The Hard Road Will Take You Home*, you'll feel the same way too.

Introduction

ENDEAVOUR THROUGH ADVERSITY

Here we go. I'm in The Badlands now…

I was part of an elite military group operating in the desert under the cover of darkness, preparing to engage a group of militia leaders. My heart was pounding. This would be my first gunfight as a tier one operator having worked through Selection, the gruelling 'job interview' required to thrive within the UK's specialized fighting forces – a squadron of expert operators that served in the world's most hostile environments – where I'd shown that I was in possession of the physical and psychological grit needed to excel under pressure. While training had provided a taster for the intense, against-all-odds operations I'd be expected to complete, the action when it arrived was an eye-opener.

The battle had been planned to the nth degree; no detail had been spared and my role in the mission was to operate as a sniper. Moving purposefully but quietly somewhere near the front of the group, my adrenaline spiked. I was fired up, I knew exactly where I had to be when the shooting kicked off and what I had to do, as did everyone else in the team. Meanwhile, the enemy was none the wiser. This was it: *Everything you've trained for, Staz... Just focus.* I listened to the radio chatter through my comms and every now and then an eerie *whoomph* trembled in the darkness around us – the dull echo of an explosion rippling somewhere else in the valley.

When the scrapping broke out for real, the group around me seemed to move as a fluid unit, taking up their pre-arranged positions and picking off the enemy one-by-one. I saw hostile gunmen crumpling to the floor in the chaos. Shocked awake in the darkness, they had taken up defensive positions and were fighting back aggressively, but their bullets seemed to whistle away into the shadows. *Close, but not close enough.* When an explosion ripped through the air near my position, I watched as a mud and stone wall collapsed and every sense seemed to malfunction at once – I couldn't see, hear, speak, or even smell. I'd gone numb too. My mouth had been open at the time of the blast. Had I been clenching my jaw, there's every chance both eardrums would have been ruptured by the intense overpressure. Later, when the operation was concluded, we returned to base to discuss what had happened in a 'hot debrief'. By the sounds of it, the mission had been a massive success.

'Fucking hell, that was amazing,' I thought. 'That's the *Call of Duty* shit I'd had in mind when I signed up for this.'

Interestingly, nobody else seemed to care about the excitement and pride I was experiencing in the aftermath; nobody knew that in the controlled chaos, I'd experienced a powerful increase in confidence at being able to stick to the battle plan that had been laid out. Or, as the battle rocked and convulsed around me, how I'd successfully leant upon several key techniques, tactics and procedures picked up from combat training. I'd also felt a huge sense of purpose by fighting alongside a group of expert operators, and our bond, established through teamwork and camaraderie, had kept everyone in the group alive. Finally, I'd recalled several hard lessons from my military career – phrases, ideas and reminders picked up from senior operators, or the Directing Staff (DS) overseeing the brutal Selection process. In the scrap, these cues had boosted my confidence. They'd told me I could survive in a situation where the odds were most definitely stacked against me.

Ego is the enemy.

How we do anything is how we do everything.

Endeavour through adversity.

These realizations were pivotal. I now knew from first-hand experience that:

1. When an operator was exposed to a full-on operation, the values of battle prep would deliver success.
2. The techniques, tactics and procedures learned in training would keep me going, especially when the physical and emotional suffering felt overwhelming, or when self-discipline became a life-or-death requirement.
3. When the rockets and rounds tore through the air, and my brothers scrapped around me, the power of teamwork was brought to bear.
4. The theories and concepts that had been screamed at me

during training drills could be sharpened into something more tangible.

When brought together, these lessons and skills allowed me to thrive under pressure, innovate in terrifying situations and achieve during chaotic events where many other men and women would have crumbled and died.

But this was only just the beginning.

* * *

Fast-forward to 2018. I was leaving the military and launching the technical clothing start-up, ThruDark, with my friend and fellow elite operator, Louis Tinsley. This was a field in which I possessed zero experience and yet the same principles I'd used in elite service would weirdly help me to develop and grow until ThruDark was regarded a massive success. Skills and know-how that had once steadied me during gunfights and extreme survival events proved equally applicable to business, innovation and enterprise when the pressure was on. I used them as motivational ideas and practical jumping-off points in an environment that, at times, felt as daunting and unsettling as my early days in the war business.

Let me explain how I got there in the first place. In 2005, I joined the Royal Marines Commandos where I later went on to pass the Royal Marines Sniper Course. Nobody in my family had served in the military before, so this was something I felt particularly proud of. Then in 2008, I signed up for Selection with the military elite and for the next ten years I served at the sharpest end of combat as a sergeant, sniper and demolitions expert, and later a multi-skilled sniper instructor. Due to my involvement in a number of risky operations in battle, I was awarded the Conspicuous Gallantry Cross for combat. However, once my time with the squadron was done, I decided to explore my options beyond the military. Getting a job in personal security – a logical vocation for many former operators – seemed too safe, too boring. (By the way, I'm not knocking those individuals that have gone into that line of work. It's a solid gig.) But testing myself in an area where the creative risks and emotional rewards felt potentially bigger, *next level*, seemed like a step in line with my military career. I wanted to push myself beyond what might have been reasonably expected of me and was ready to turn the page.

This was the first time I'd ever been required to consider my life beyond active service and it felt like a minefield. Up until that moment, my work-life balance had been intense, but rewarding, though the effort required to survive had taken its toll. I'd lost friends to IED blasts. I'd even seen the gruesome result of an explosion when a dog picked through the gore-splattered aftermath and emerged with a victim's dick in its mouth. Still, none of these incidents compared to the time I'd slipped on a clump of slimy goo during a night operation. In the dark, it was impossible to discern exactly what I'd walked into. Then, once the building had been cleared, I went back to check on the mess with a torch and discovered to my horror that I'd stepped through what was left of an enemy gunman's brain.

As I looked to the future, I knew a change was needed. At the time I was thirty-three years old. My first marriage had failed and I was two years into a new relationship. I didn't want to make the same mistakes twice.

'Mate, you've still got plenty of gas in the tank,' I thought. 'What do you want to do?'

Around the same time, Louis was standing at the very same crossroads. After scrapping as an operator for eight years, his back wasn't great and he'd been forced to retire through injury. I'd first met Louis having joined the Royal Marines with 40 Commando, Bravo Company, and the pair of us became close friends, though we never actually fought alongside one another. Like me, Louis was ready for a new challenge and we had plenty in common. Both of us had taken a great deal of pride in our appearance and personal admin as operators – looking 'the part' was a big deal. Both of us appreciated the value of functional kit, tech and safety, which was vital when operating in extreme environments, such as the desert, where temperatures could reach 50 degrees Celsius, or the mountains, where a ripped glove, damaged boot or inappropriate clothing could lead to frostbite and death.

Meanwhile, I'd heard from a number of former operators working in the extreme adventure business that a lot of the kit being used wasn't exactly bombproof. That's when Louis and I stumbled across an idea. *Could we deliver something different to the market – the type of clothing suitable for both elite adventurers and casual explorers?* We undoubtedly had the credibility to front such a project. *But did we have the business acumen?* We also had the expertise to appreciate the value of functional clothing because in war our lives and the survival of everybody around us had depended upon it. *Was it possible to translate those high standards into fully developed and marketable products?*

The answer was very much *yes*, and together we established ThruDark – a clothing company that enmeshed the military elite's ethos into a line of technically innovative kit, the type required for incredibly challenging environments. We're talking remote mountains, deserts and frozen, end-of-the-earth outposts where only the brave would dare to tread. The clothing we had in mind had to be highly advanced and functional, as our kit had been during our time in the military elite. *It also had to look badass.*

At times, the work felt daunting – we were breaking new ground after all – but it was in those moments that I came to rely upon the processes used in combat. *ThruDark was a clothing start-up, but it operated very much like an elite military unit.* And during our early days, we applied the philosophies usually associated with battle prep, by working through business plans, projections, designs and tests, where everything was assessed through a military-style viewfinder. In the process, Louis and I worked with meticulous detail, conducting 'pre-mortems' on potential pitfalls and the cost of failure, and using recon skills to locate the right materials, suppliers and distributors. Meanwhile, debriefs, plus the lessons learned within them, were conducted under a harsh spotlight – mistakes were examined and evaluated with a view that screw-ups would happen from time to time, *but if we failed we would fail forward.*

Techniques, tactics and procedure also played a part, and as we learned new skills in a new industry, I began to take inspiration from battle-borne practices, such as how to control the controllables, or the importance of building an armoury of daily habits that would help me to locate stability in flashpoints or moments of stress. As a result, the age-old struggle with production disputes and creative differences, looming deadlines and financial migraines were negotiated in much the same way I'd processed a gun battle, a fast-rope descent on to a moving vessel, or the injury to a teammate. By putting one foot in front of the other and acting with purpose and rational thought we were able to sidestep most of the emotional pitfalls and financial IEDs.

As the company grew and our workforce expanded, ThruDark embraced the power of teamwork and unity; we accepted our inexperience in certain areas; we realized that left-field thinking should be encouraged at all times. At the same time it was decided that our successes had to be observed, but not overly celebrated, because that wasn't how we did things in the military. Finally, ThruDark relied upon the hard lessons and sayings delivered by military life, such as *'That'll do will never do'* and *'Medals are for mothers'*. These cues had kept us alive in service, as evidenced by my intense first battle, but they also served to remind us of the spirit that had led us to success in the past and would therefore do so again. Three years on, those values have established ThruDark as a leading force in a specialist market. The company now stands as an example of what can happen when elite discipline meets creative effort.

All of this brings us to *The Hard Road Will Take You Home – What the Military Elite Teaches Us About Innovation, Endeavour and Next Level Success*. You'll soon realize that this is not a straightforward memoir. Instead it's a book that distils the processes and tactics I've gathered throughout my career and translates them into tools (*'Action Ons'*) that can be used in any number of settings, and by individuals with a wide range of experience and backgrounds. Really anyone looking to innovate, show creativity or handle adversity will find value here, whether that be in business, family, sport, personal relationships or when embarking on a gruelling life challenge, such as overcoming a serious injury or working towards a physical or psychological milestone.

For example, the concept of *never above you, never below you, always beside you* was a phrase used to underscore the value of team unity. It suggested that everyone working within a group was of equal value, there for one another in shit times. Elsewhere, one of the most impactful lessons I picked up in service would come to inspire the title of this book. When I first heard the phrase 'The hard road will take you home', I was around twenty-five weeks into the Royal Marines basic training course and my group was breaking up for a summer leave period. We had been ordered to the Bottom Field, which, as any seasoned commando will tell you, plays home to the infamous assault course and is where most of the physical punishments are dished out. This day was no different, and as a parting gift we were subjected to a competitive session between the troops, which involved a series of dead lifts, car pulls and excruciating body weight exercises.

After a mauling from the PTIs that seemed to last the whole day, the group was gathered together for a briefing. These were to be the motivational words that we were supposed to take with us through leave and beyond, and they were designed to make an impact as we stood out at the bottom of a grassy knoll. At the top, a bunch of hierarchy types had gathered together and were looking down on us from their perch. In those days, I was still getting used to the military ranking system, so the authority of some of the senior figures in attendance was lost on me, though the stars, pips and crowns on their clothing told me enough. *They were pretty important.*

Suddenly the whistles blew and everyone stood to attention. We were being addressed.

'The Colonel's going to say some words,' shouted a voice. Though really, the colonel in question needed little in the way of introduction. He was a man who carried a serious reputation. He was also the type of character that demanded respect on appearance alone: a man mountain, albeit a little wiry, he swaggered with authority and his face looked weathered, as if he'd lived and thrived in a career built on adversity.

'He's nails,' I thought. 'I wouldn't want to get in a tear-up with him.'

This powerful impression was cemented further once he had opened his mouth to address us.

'*Men!*' His voice boomed across the Bottom Field like an old-school cannon going off. The entire troop seemed to inhale at once. You could have heard a pin drop.

'Let me tell you that the endeavour you're currently enduring in Royal Marines' training is the best thing that you can be doing in order to strive towards your goals for a greater purpose. You are joining an important brotherhood, one that will define your life in battle and beyond.

'You will suffer hardship,' he continued. 'There's little doubt about that. The most important thing is that you should never take the easy option. Don't ever look to cut corners in anything you do. Finally, remember this: *The hard road will take you home.*'

'Wow,' I thought, 'that is brilliant.'

Exactly why it resonated so deeply will remain a mystery. Perhaps it was something to do with the fact that for much of my life I'd felt as if I was walking the hard road. I'd certainly been working tirelessly to move forward. I also took a lot of pride in the fact that I was able to push through moments of physical pain and emotional suffering in order to grow as an individual. As you'll soon discover, I'd figured out at an early age that discomfort would define me in one way or another and it was all about endeavour through adversity as far as I was concerned. That speech ensured that the idea of taking the path of most resistance would stay with me for life.

It followed me into service, where I'd be ordered to perform painful training exercises or to clean my kit. Rather than going through the motions, I'd think, 'Right, don't opt for the easy option, let's knuckle down here.' There were times on drills or during time trials on Selection when I would have been forgiven for taking my foot off the gas, having already done enough to qualify, but I pushed myself even harder. I would come to learn quite quickly that this was an essential trait of the elite operator: I needed to go the extra yard at all times, I had to focus on the finer details, and when war became ugly it was my time to pull the straps on my backpack a little tighter and think, 'Fuck it, I'm cracking on.' I later brought this attitude into my career beyond the military by refusing to clock out until my work was done.

Throughout *The Hard Road Will Take You Home* I'll walk you through four concepts that make up the life of an elite operator. These are: battle prep; techniques, tactics and procedures; teamwork; and the lessons we should all consider when learning how to innovate, persevere and succeed. When I left the military elite to start a new life with ThruDark, a lot of my friends thought I was making a bad move. They couldn't believe I'd left active service for a start-up company with next to no experience in business. They expected me to struggle. They reckoned on me screwing up. They wondered if I'd come out of the experience feeling just as psychologically battered and bruised as I would a military tour. They weren't alone though. I was feeling exactly the same way. The difference was that I'd wanted to embrace the unknown because throughout my career I'd constantly been told that nothing would come easily and pain was an expected companion to victory. I was ready for that pain due to the fact I had the tools to overcome it – and to succeed.

As a book, *The Hard Road Will Take You Home* encapsulates that spirit and arrives stacked with insight, easily applicable techniques and psychological processes gathered from my time serving with the most resilient fighting force in the world.

As a creative resource, *it's a weapon.*

PART ONE

BATTLE PREP

BRIEFING

Preparation was everything in war. Rarely did an elite military operation happen without a plan, and in advance of any attack, a specialized fighting force was readied tactically, mentally and militarily. Nothing was left to chance in my line of work because everything was fast-moving, highly unpredictable and, without overegging the narrative, fucking dangerous. To run into an occupied village, all guns blazing, without thought or purpose, was the fastest track to an unpleasant end.

For that reason the whats, whys and wherefores of every mission were detailed in advance – and often with an excruciatingly high level of detail. On a short-term level this was particularly important: I had to run around in the dark during most battles, as explosions and screams went off left, right and centre. The work could be daunting and ultra-violent. It exposed me to some pretty harrowing sights and without a clear plan in place I might have failed. However, in the grander scheme of things, a readied mind and an overarching mission structure was vital. It kept me motivated and focused; it prevented me from experiencing confusion or shock.

How the UK's military elite runs through its battle prep is one of the reasons why it stands apart from so many other expert fighting forces across the world. Selection had readied my body and brain for service, though I certainly remember being taken aback by the orders process for my first-ever operation. During a lengthy meeting, the team's roles were clearly defined, there was no doubting exactly what had to be done and by whom, and anyone who felt unsure of even the slightest detail was given the space and freedom to put up their hands and say so. Nobody was mocked for asking a question that might help to keep one or all of us alive.

Battle prep wasn't just about tactics and maps, though, and I later learned that a lot of combat readiness was existential. For example, many high-profile missions required a leap of faith at some point, a moment where my team would commit to the mission, or some incredibly dangerous attack. But those decisions were never taken blindly. They were always backed by gathered intelligence, analysis and a confidence born of experience and training. Psychologically, as elite operators we also understood that our future results weren't defined by any past screw-ups. Instead, we were encouraged to regard our mistakes as building blocks for success – lessons that could help us to improve, or reminders that we'd failed in the past and risen up stronger. Acceptance meant we would do so again during moments of adversity.

On a more practical level, the military elite employed several idea-generating techniques that were used in order to a) locate an enemy's weakness, and b) turn the spotlight internally so that any flaws in our own practices could be revealed. When it came to the strategies required for dealing with both, everything we did was then executed with willingness, diligence and a commitment to excellence. Overall, these techniques helped me to prepare for war, but I later realized that many of them could be translated into the concepts of business, teamwork and leadership, and without too much fuss. It was an important discovery: in everyday work or missions, important details and events are often left unplanned, and by too many people. It's for this very reason that you should consider battle prep as a game-changing resource…

1

INTO THE DARK
(THE LEAP OF FAITH)

All of us are required to take a leap of faith from time to time, whether that's in our business or personal lives. It might be that we've come up with an actionable idea that requires a risky financial investment, or we've pushed for a new kind of career altogether. Or maybe we've decided to start a new life abroad or retrain in an entirely unfamiliar field. None of these decisions come easily; the work required to succeed can be painful and throughout there will be dark nights of the soul, moments of self-doubt and a hell of a lot of fear.

I know these feelings all too well because I experienced them, both literally – having thrown myself from a plane on a number of night operations – and figuratively, when starting ThruDark. Luckily, I'd been schooled for challenging events throughout my military career in what felt like a never-ending succession of tests – leaps of faith that prepared me for elite service. The mindset instilled by my progress became the glue that would help bring ThruDark into existence, but this same glue can be applied to many forms of civilian endeavour, as I'll explain…

Parachute failure!

I plummeted to the deck, my half-opened canopy flapping and flailing like a plastic shopping bag tumbling along a city road. G-forces yanked my body to and fro; my oxygen mask was wrenched to one side and my left arm seemed pinned to my ribs by gravity. Everywhere was chaos. I watched the black of sky and the tangled, twisted lines that connected my harness to a now collapsed 'chute as the world tumbled over and over, round and round. It was as if I'd been dropped into the capsule of a fairground waltzer as it pitched and yawed, only this ride was turbocharged and potentially fatal. Rational thought and methodical action, I realized, was suddenly everything. If I couldn't cut away the flapping bag of linen above me with the pull of a cord, I'd be seen off in a very messy, though blessedly swift ending.

'Don't flap, mate,' I told myself. *'Don't fucking flap…'*

Really, I should have had it in me to wriggle out of what seemed to be a fairly routine parachute failure. Compared to some of the many scrapes I'd experienced in war, in which I'd come close to being shot dead, or detonated into pieces by an IED, this was a situation that granted me a certain amount of control. I knew my canopy would open fully if I could untangle the twisted lines above; a reserve 'chute also gave me a fairly solid fallback position. Struggling against gravity, I freed both hands and grabbed at the risers, kicking out my legs in opposite directions like a frog. I'd been told during countless drills that by generating enough violent force it was possible to correct the twisted lines – unless, of course, I was really unlucky. As I kicked around, the situation didn't seem to be improving. My lines were still tangled and a worrying realization dawned upon me.

By the looks of things, I'd been really unlucky.

How had it come to this? My jump that night had been a training effort, not a serious operation: a full mission profile, in which the operators involved were expected to land on a designated landing zone (LZ) with the type of kit normally required for a real-time job. A large bag had been slung between my legs. I was set with a weapon, my sniper rifle and helmet; my body had been weighed down by ammo, ballistic plates, radios and night vision goggles. As the plane moved above our target, the unit had stacked up in the back, ready to swoop into the darkness before opening our 'chutes and, at that moment, everything seemed to be in order. I'd run an equipment check and double-check beforehand. Then I'd checked and double-checked everything again. *I was good.* The light at the back of the plane glowed green. *It was go time.* I'd then watched as my teammates plunged forwards until it was my turn... And I stepped off the tail ramp and dropped into the sky, scooping at the air around me with my hands in order to maintain a firm body position as I fell. For a second, everything was silent and still. Then the air began buffeting around me as I gathered velocity. Before long the wind resistance had built into a roaring hurricane as I plummeted down, down, down, while a methodical countdown ticked over in my head...

One thousand.

Two thousand.

Three thousand...

The type of parachutes I'd been trained to use were pretty big and normally took around eight seconds to fully open, but in those first few moments I became locked in a violent struggle.

G-forces twisted my body and there was no way to lift my head or to check on what was happening with the 'chute above me.

Four thousand.

Five thousand.

Six thousand…

Something was off. I was falling quicker than I should have been, though there was some reassurance in the fact that I wasn't yet free-falling – there was a little drag in the air around me, which meant that my canopy had partially opened, but then I caught a glimpse of the fabric above. I'd experienced a seriously unfortunate break, a kit malfunction, and given that untwisting the lines by kicking and thrashing wasn't going to work, I had no other choice but to attempt a cut-away of the main canopy before releasing the reserve. This was easier said than done, however. Firstly, I'd have to pull the release cord to cut away from the main 'chute. Secondly, I'd have to yank at another to release the backup. Then, in a moment of almost comical timing, my jacket zip failed, ripped open and billowed about my face. I was suddenly blinded.

'Fucking hell, this isn't good,' I thought. 'I'm losing altitude. I need to make a move on my reserve 'chute and fast…'

The calm I'd enjoyed moments earlier was fast evaporating. But we all knew the risks that accompanied a role in the military elite and nobody was in any doubt that your time could be up at any moment – in training or conflict. *Was this mine?* I wrestled with my 'chute, but the velocity and wind resistance pummelling my body were becoming increasingly powerful, which meant the chances of my wriggling free were shortening considerably. I felt nauseous and close to blacking out – everything seemed out of control. My left hand clasped around the yellow handle connected to my upper left chest, which I knew would jettison my main canopy, but I also needed to pull at the red handle to release the reserve. When I looked down, it was only a foot away from my face but reaching for it was a serious effort – the pressures being exerted upon me were too strong. Essentially, I was arm-wrestling with gravity. Meanwhile, the other lads in the unit had seen me falling through the sky as their canopies opened up. I later learned that they'd been trying to raise me on the comms, but my antennae had been ripped away as I'd spiralled through the air. Like me, they guessed my time was slipping away. I only had a second or two to take positive action.

I tensed and flexed, pulling at the yellow cord and hoping for the best. Instantly, my main parachute ripped away and I was free-falling, accelerating towards the ground. One, two, three seconds passed as I arched my spine, set the legs and head back and reached forward in order to maintain a strong body shape in the air. I then punched my right hand forward aggressively, freeing my arm from the clutches of gravity and yanked at the red cord. There was a heavy tug. The reserve canopy blossomed open and I lurched upwards, feeling the reassuring drag of wind resistance. I experienced a huge sense of relief.

The adrenaline burning through me seemed to cool a little as I reassessed my situation. I had to reboot. First things first: *was everything still working?* I took control of the parachute risers and ran through a series of checks. The positives: I could move to the left and to the right; I was able to break and flare; everything was still operational.

'Well, I won't be landing in a ball of hurt,' I thought.

The negatives: I had to work out where I was. Given the darkness it was impossible to guess at my position, or to pick out any recognizable features, or teammates, on the ground below. By the looks of things I was going to be well short of the LZ. The only question was: *by how much?*

I quickly located the correct bearing and pulled my knees into a tuck position in order to reduce the wind resistance around me. I then altered the canopy's drive and surged towards the LZ. My aim was to shave away as many running metres between my teammates and me as possible, and I picked a spot between two rural outbuildings and swooped between them gracefully, sprinting into an area of cover. I spun my canopy around, performed a quick search of the area for any mock hostiles and fixed the radio. It was probably my most impressive landing on the job, ever. *Oh, the irony.*

Then I slumped down on my bag, sparked up a smoke and thanked Lady Luck. I'd held my nerve, my training had worked, though there was little doubt I'd experienced a fortunate escape.

The leaps of faith I experienced in the military tended to be very literal – I jumped from planes, abseiled away from cliff tops and buildings, and tombstoned into freezing, churning seas. But all of us have to take equally daunting tests from time to time and yours could be something entirely different. Maybe your business is making a transition into the digital financial age? Or perhaps you've chosen to accept a project or challenge that's almost guaranteed to stretch you and your team to their absolute limits?

The emotions associated with those experiences are really no different to the ones I felt when wrestling with a half-opened parachute, or having stepped into a gunfight. (Though they are undoubtedly amplified in war.) Exposure to trepidation, fear, stress and a level of anxiety regarding the 'what if…?s' is common. How you control those feelings is usually the decisive factor between success and failure.

Of course, nobody steps into events of this kind knowing exactly what to do or how to succeed. *By their very nature leaps of faith are unknowns.* However, the military taught me that they can be approached in a step-by-step basis and I later applied that attitude to the development of ThruDark. For example, as a wet-behind-the-ears Royal Marines recruit entering into basic training, I was a *know nothing*, but so was everybody else around me, and any recruit claiming otherwise (and there were one or two) was a bullshitter. The truth was that nobody stepping into the gymnasium for their first ever bleep test – dressed in white shorts, vest and plimsolls – understood what it really took to crawl across a muddy battlefield as grenades and bullets exploded around them. War seemed a million miles away. But by following instructions and displaying discipline and determination throughout what was one of the toughest military training programmes in the world, most recruits would get there because the work was designed to build warriors in a series of progressive tests. And each one pushed a potential Marine past what they'd initially considered possible. Eventually we were transformed into fully functional military assets, capable of scrapping it out in some of the most brutal hellholes on earth.

Parachute training was a case in point. When I started with

the Marines, the very thought of throwing myself out of a plane was exciting but overwhelming. *How the hell would it all work?* I really had no idea. Handily, the system forced every recruit to accept the psychological pressures and physical rigours of taking on such an action. There were briefings, courses and training sessions on land until, eventually, we were taken up in a military plane with an instructor, who then jumped into the sky while demonstrating the various drills, body positions and manoeuvres required to operate the 'chute. At that point, everything was new. My mind went into a spin.

You're jumping out of a plane at night – are you nuts?

What the fuck are you doing?

What's going to happen when I do this for real?

Through process, and with repeated practice and training, those thoughts soon faded into the background, as they often do with any leap of faith. Before long, I'd completed enough jumps for the work to become second nature. I was no longer thinking about my basic body position, or equipment. Instead I ran through my checks – my altimeter, watch and bearings – because it had been drilled into me to do so and it really wasn't too dissimilar to learning to drive. As a learner, everything feels like a sensory overload, but time and practice usually brings a level of confidence, which then creates competence.

It also helped that during those first few months with the Royal Marines I'd been trained to stay increasingly *risk aware*. In dangerous and violent situations, I knew how to remain calm while functioning effectively. Later, when I progressed through training, active service and then Selection, I constantly played off the risks of what I was doing against the rewards. That allowed me to think coolly under pressure and operate to the best of my ability, especially during intense and chaotic events. Anyone not of a military background watching me as I moved into a heavily guarded enemy compound might have questioned my sanity. The truth was that I'd been hard-wired to take those actions, *to make those leaps of faith*, not without a little fear or doubt, but a deep-rooted understanding of the controllables and my own capabilities.

It's not a stretch to say that a similar mindset was required when establishing ThruDark in 2017. In fact, everything about starting a company felt like a massive leap of faith. At that time I didn't have a clue about setting up a business, let alone one that could be loosely described as a 'clothing brand'. (Albeit a clothing brand with a highly technical spin.) The very thought of it was intimidating as our plans began to take shape, but like a new Marine taking on their first parachute jump, I realized it was important to listen to instruction from business associates, take notes of the lessons I was learning and have confidence in the process. In much the same way that I'd readied my kit before a parachute jump, checking it and then double-checking it and studying the landing zone and operational details in advance, so I assessed the risks of what we were planning to do while preparing myself for our launch into the unknown.

Then Louis and I went for it.

Firstly, we confirmed our overall concept: the launch of a technical clothing start-up. The idea was rock solid and it had stemmed from the career-long importance of looking after my equipment, most pressingly my weapon systems, though the thought had first been drummed into me once I'd been installed at the Royal Marines Commando Training Centre in Lympstone. There I was taught a vital rule: I always had to consider *my weapon, my kit, myself* – and in that order. This was pretty standard stuff I knew, and the importance of such a determination was self-evident from the off. *My weapon*: because no soldier wanted their hardware to jam during a gunfight. *My kit*: because good husbandry, especially regarding the maintenance of clothing and equipment, was vital when functioning in hostile situations. *Myself*: because the environment could be a dangerous enemy at times, where skin rot, infected cuts and dysentery had the potential to be every bit as debilitating as a mortar strike or ambush.

More often than not, the equipment issued to us was fit for purpose, especially within the elite units of the British military, but that didn't mean there wasn't any room for improvement. Poorly fitting or uncomfortable kit was often tinkered with, or doctored for better use, and I first spotted these alterations taking place having passed out with the Royal Marines in 2006. I'd been sent up to Glen Coe in Scotland to join with 40 Commando, Bravo Company for mountain training where the weather was terrible. As we gathered together I noticed that a lot of lads were amending their clothing to make it more resistant to the wet and the cold. Some of them had sewn Arctic socks into the sleeves of their windproof smock jackets as an extra layer of protection. Others threaded wire into the hoods of their jackets to ensure they held firm against the high winds.

This MO was taken up a notch when I started on Selection in 2008, where the attitude among the students – as the volunteering candidates are known – was more akin to that of a professional sports team. Given the intense competition for a spot with the military elite, every individual on the brutal course looked for their edge, no matter how small, and kit tinkering was one way of getting there. The idea was that a couple of padded straps on a hopeful's Bergen would deliver some respite from the pain and therefore create a critical advantage during the timed runs that took place in the Hills Phase. Other students added pockets to their belts for different pieces of kit (such as water bottles) or affixed a compass pocket so their navigation device was readily accessible during the more pressurized drills. These tweaks might have seemed minor, or even pointless, but in the heat of an intense exercise, they sometimes proved the difference between one student coping ably and another running around with his head on fire at the worst possible moment.

The need for clothing maintenance was probably most evident during my time as a sniper. Within the military, specialist marksmen were regarded as *kit pests* – dudes who obsessed over the appearance and functionality of their equipment, mainly because our very survival depended upon it as we stalked through all manner of terrain to observe and then neutralize an enemy target. This was painful work, though we were prepared for the effort. As a taster of what the sniping life held in store, during training I was forced to crawl on my belt buckle through the gorse and undergrowth of Woodbury Common in East Devon. When I returned to base my body was often covered in painful cuts and rashes, and I noticed that a lot of trainee snipers had taken to sewing patches over their knees, shins and thighs to protect them from the spiteful undergrowth. Mainly this was repurposed, heavy-duty material ripped from an old canvas tent. Larger patches were even stitched into the arse of our standard issue trousers, which was a godsend when tasked with sitting in the firing position for hours on end. Thanks to these tweaks, lying in ambush was made a little more bearable.

When it came to self-preservation, however, the importance of camouflage and concealment was drilled into us from the very off, particularly the processes required to hide our weapons, and ourselves. (In other words: blending into the background without alerting the enemy to our presence.) A glinting gun sight or rattling equipment might give away a sniper's position and place an operation in jeopardy, so once inserted into the field, snipers tended to amend their kit and equipment with a fastidious eye for detail. I was forever dipping bits of clothing into dye, or spraying it in various colours, depending on whether I was operating in an urban or outdoors environment; I added cantilevers to my weapon and applied red dots here and there which helped me to sight the target quickly and more effectively at closer ranges. These were minor adjustments, but much in the same way that an F1 team will spend ages (and hundreds of thousands of pounds in development money) to improve the aerodynamics of a wing mirror, or the weight of a steering wheel in order to increase the car's speed by a minimal percentage, these tweaks often reaped big rewards.

This attention to detail would later propel me into an exciting new world with ThruDark – *the leap of faith* – and to ready myself for the experience, I threw up a whiteboard in the front room of my house. I then took my cue from the NATO sequence of orders (which I'll explain in detail shortly), as Louis and I laid out a very loose five-year plan and set a clear vision for design, development and launch. We studied the market, assessed our competitors and worked out our typical buyer, plus the type of profit margins we hoped to achieve. Then the name arrived. *ThruDark* was a saying taken from our experiences in the military where we'd had to work through a series of grim and arduous challenges. The title also stood to represent anyone who was enduring a personal hardship of their own. Our eventual slogan, *Endeavour Through Adversity*, matched that same idea: as far as we were concerned it was applicable to both our journey into business and our time in the military.

Having been emboldened by the planning phase, we then decided to put our foot on the accelerator. At that point I was still seeing out my final months with the squadron, but Louis had been medically discharged and had some time to kill.

'Fuck it, I'm taking my balls in my hand,' he said one day. 'I'm going to China, on a recon mission for materials and factories...'

Louis had spotted a unique business opportunity. It had recently been announced that one of the biggest textile trade fairs in the world was taking place at Guangzhou, but the adventure was loaded with risk. At the time, China was on the red list for travel. British military types weren't allowed to enter, especially those that were specialized assets. Louis could expect to be in trouble if his background was discovered. That would have landed him in a grubby jail cell for a very long time, though as far as Louis was concerned, it was a risk worth taking. With some online research, he registered himself as a guest at the trade fair.

A few weeks later, he was working his way across the convention floor. Louis picked up fabric samples and dished out our newly made ThruDark business cards. Within weeks we'd received one or two pieces of prototype kit and hastily put together designs. But everything was a mess: the arms were too short on the coats; the legs were too big on the trousers; on some garments, the pockets had been stitched into the wrong place. As far as our leap of faith was concerned, we were away from the plane and free-falling; counting down the seconds and waiting for our 'chute to open.

Eventually it did – *thank God*. We secured a substantial investment from a personal friend and business investor, and Louis and I set to work, developing our brand with cutting-edge materials, before personally battle-testing our products in the harshest environments. Throughout this process we were assisted by individuals attuned to a life lived at extreme levels – the Olympic cyclist, Victoria Pendleton CBE, the former SBS operator and TV presenter, Jason Fox, and the England rugby captain, Dylan Hartley. They all gave us feedback on our latest product drops.

With the world-record-breaking mountain climber, Nims Purja MBE, ThruDark even developed an extreme cold weather summit suit. Our prototype was used as Nims climbed all fourteen Death Zone* mountains in six months during the world-record-breaking *Project Possible* expeditions of 2019. In 2021, Nims then led a team of Nepalese climbers to the first ever ascent of K2 in winter while wearing an improved ThruDark suit in temperatures of minus 75 degrees Celsius. Every millimetre of his clothing had to be bombproofed. At sea level, a torn pocket zip could be considered annoying. A torn pocket zip while

---

* Death Zone mountains are the peaks set at 8,000 metres above sea level, where the air is perilously thin and a mountaineer can expect to die if they hang around without bottled oxygen for too long.

climbing 8,000 metres above in hurricane force winds would probably prove fatal. Fumbling with a knackered pocket would need a climber to take off his mitts. Using only his inner gloves in deadly temperatures would lead to frostbite. Frostbite would then prevent that climber from moving up or down on the mountain and they would be left to freeze to death.

Due to our uncompromising designs, Nims's kit held strong. And three financial years on from our 2019 launch, and after a series of mistakes, hard lessons and psychologically testing flashpoints, ThruDark made a profit large enough for our venture to be considered incredibly successful.

We had landed.

ACTION ON
Preparation Drills

The processes applied to the creation of ThruDark were hardly unique; they'd been developed in military training and, as far as I was concerned, seemed perfectly translatable to civilian industry. In order to start a business, Louis and I had to first take a leap of faith, but it was a leap of faith we could prepare for. We didn't rush blindly in by making bold statements about our plans. Neither of us accepted mass orders for product before we were ready. We knew that setting up a fancy website without having a portfolio of kit that we were happy with was a potentially damaging step too. Instead, we exposed ourselves to a series of educational events and underwent the business equivalent of a Royal Marines basic training course. Running risk assessments, taking recon missions to China and stepping out of our respective comfort zones was no different – psychologically at least – to crawling through the mud in a mock battle, or performing a series of sprints in a fitness test. We were preparing ourselves for the bigger challenges ahead.

And you can do the same.

Don't believe me? Well, imagine a frustrated office worker looking to establish their own business. They've got a great idea, they possess the skills to turn that idea into a living wage, and, long term, their standard of living is likely to improve as a result of such a change. Sure, they *could* quit their nine-to-five the very morning after arriving at their decision, but that would present a massive risk, a bit like parachuting out of a plane without first running through the necessary safety protocols. Instead they should approach their leap of faith by taking a number of precautionary steps, which might include:

* Chatting to friends, colleagues or family members who have taken a similar career step. This will give them an idea of what to expect and the pitfalls to avoid.

* Preparing a financial safety net in advance of their transition to shield them from any major monetary turbulence.

* Researching the basics of their new business in advance. Exploring the necessary equipment, staffing issues, premises and tax requirements will help them to hit the ground running.

* Developing a vision for how the business should look in the coming years by running a NATO-style sequence of orders. In our case, this ran as follows:
  ○ **Preliminaries**: We checked the market we were moving into. *Was this an area primed for growth?*
  ○ **Situation**: We were fresh out of the military and on the verge of starting a new company.
  ○ **Mission**: To launch our first line of products.
  ○ **Execution**: We would design, test, produce and sell our new range.

○ **Service and support:** We'd need to rely heavily on an outside investor for financial help and advice in the early stages.

○ **Commands and signals:** *How would we communicate our plans to one another, and the market, in the early stages?* We used the whiteboard in my front room for internal organization and social media platforms as a brand development tool.

Of course, these processes won't magic away the overall scale of the task in hand overnight. Jumping out of a plane at a great height is still a risky endeavour, no matter how many safety drills have been conducted in advance. Having said that, with the correct amount of training and preparation, a leap of faith can feel manageable and less susceptible to disaster. We only have to ready ourselves and remember two words.

Don't flap.

DEBRIEF

- Leaps of faith are supposed to be scary, so don't feel overwhelmed by the fact that you're feeling fear or anxiety when making a massive change, or stepping out of your comfort zone.

- Intimidating events can be prepared for by taking smaller steps towards the overall objective. It might be that you need to discipline a team member at work but dislike the thought of confrontation. Work yourself up to the event by war gaming the scenario with a friend or loved one.

- Acknowledge your progress. As you take your leap of faith and advance towards your ultimate objective, look back to the person you were when the mission started. If you've adopted the step-by-step approach you'll feel pleasantly shocked at how much you've improved.

2

REDEFINE YOUR DISASTERS

We were regarded as the best of the best in UK military terms, but we were also self-described bastard sons of illegitimate parents, and pretty much everyone in tier one service had overcome extreme hardship, either in the line of fire, or because of some other challenging life event. Many of us were fuck-ups or had fucked up in some way. What set us apart from the ordinary soldier was that every operator had learned to move past those negative events in order to grow and progress.

For example, some of the lads I knew had survived a troubled background. As a result they'd taught themselves to withstand extreme psychological and physical discomfort. Others had experienced personal failure, or disaster, but had rebounded in such a way that hardcore discipline had become their stabilizing force.

These narratives are not solely confined to the elite warrior, however, and all of us are a story in progress, with good and bad plot lines that define us, whether we like them or not. However, while the facts of our history are beyond our control, what we can influence is *how those plot lines affect our future. Does the former drug addict consider themselves a failure, or an individual with a powerful recovery story? Because many negative events have the potential to drive us all forward. We only have to reframe them as a positive influence...*

As a kid, I endured the types of knocks that could either break or build an individual and my story makes for grim reading. When I was seven years old my parents divorced and during the split I was wrenched away from our family home in Wigan. The upheaval felt rough and I was forced to live in Nottingham. Having changed cities and schools, I was later targeted as a bit of an outsider and a gang of older kids bullied me. They'd lie in wait whenever I stepped off the bus from school, which made the journey an emotional nightmare. Whenever my stop came into view, I'd strap down my bag just in case anything fell out during the scrapping. My school shoes were swapped for trainers, and I made sure to take off my tie, or anything else that might present a handhold. Once I'd walked into the street, the mob would emerge from the shadows, gathering around me as the daily challenge was issued: *Which one of us are you going to fight then?* Not wanting to back down, I always took my chances with the first kid in reach and having thrown one down his pipe, the others would wade in, their fists and boots flying. It was a physical and emotional battering that taught me an important lesson: life could be extremely harsh.

Things took a more horrific turn when my mum suddenly passed away from a brain haemorrhage just a few years later. She left us almost overnight and the news came as a real shock – she was only thirty-three years old. Mum spent three days on a life support machine before the decision was made to turn it off and my world suddenly imploded. I couldn't understand what was happening, or its velocity, and in the following months I found my stepdad to be a real shitbag. Thankfully I'd taken up martial arts as a way to defend myself from the local bullies and the gym became a healthy outlet for my frustrations. (Like most kids from that time, I loved Bruce Lee and took up kick-boxing.) A promising football career later looked set to earn me a professional contract and I trained with Mansfield Town, before being selected for the England Schoolboys team and trialling as a youth player with Fulham. Then, on the cusp of receiving my first professional contract, I messed around on a motocross bike with some mates and dislocated my knee in a smash. The dream of becoming a football star was over.

Given the hardships I'd endured, a life in the Royal Marines seemed ideal. I'd heard about the Commandos and knew a military career would provide a sense of purpose, some adventure and a feeling of belonging. It certainly seemed like a more exciting career step than the vocations I'd looked into during my teens, such as working as a lifeguard. In the Marines, I'd attain the attributes required to become a leader of men, such as humility, honesty and discipline. I'd push the limits of what I thought was humanly possible too, and having passed through the training phases and joined with 40 Commando, Bravo Company, my eyes were opened to an exciting new career path during what was the first of many tours to Afghanistan: *I saw the military elite in action.*

Talk about a game changer. The specialized units in the UK Armed Forces seemed so at odds with the standard green military. They looked more relaxed for a start. Around the base they wore flannel shirts and jeans; they had long hair and they carried different weapons systems and caches; and in the battlespace they seemed to come alive in chaos. Weirdly, there was very little in the way of hierarchy in their regiments, and the operators I met were clearly being encouraged to improvise, or take calculated risks in sketchy situations. Judging by the stories that got passed around base, their missions seemed to be cut with a roguish, almost rebellious streak. If the extreme sports brand Red Bull did war, they would have almost certainly sponsored the UK military elite. My mind was made up almost instantly. *I wanted to be a part of that.*

I worked towards making it into Selection, the arduous trial designed to separate those that could from those that couldn't. I wasn't a particularly big bloke. I came in at around five foot seven in height, but by reframing the disasters from my childhood I knew that I could rise up and succeed. Like my idol, Bruce Lee, I loved the idea of being an underdog; the beatings I'd endured as a kid told me I could survive conflict and physical pain, night after night; the devastating familial heartbreaks had created the layer of emotional armour that I would need to ride out any inevitable moments of debilitating doubt; and that bike crash on the eve of my dream life as a professional footballer taught me that I would need next-level discipline in everything I did. (Because not having it had shattered my knee and my sporting ambitions.) These events had seemed disastrous at the time – they *were* disastrous at the time – but I reckoned they would give me a mental advantage.

Once my interest in Selection had been piqued, I absorbed every scrap of information on the job, and learned about the type of individuals that tended to succeed, plus the sort of operations I'd be expected to execute. My obsession transformed into passion; my passion translated into an increased work ethic with the Royal Marines. I wanted to improve in every aspect of my career so I could test myself against the very best, and there was plenty in my favour. I fancied myself as being physically strong enough to last the course and I was a stubborn bastard and I functioned well in a team. My work as a sniper had also taught me how to perform under extreme pressure.

Yeah, there were doubts, though I'd had them before. As a trainee commando I occasionally experienced imposter syndrome and I'd wondered whether I really had it in me to survive in a war zone. During my first briefing on Selection, surrounded by a group of blokes who, at first glance, looked bigger, stronger and more experienced than me, those insecurities returned. *Was I fit enough? Did I have the resilience to cut it? Could I dig deep to push past my limits?* I felt a fear of failure; a fear of letting other people down. But I usually backed myself in a battle where the odds seemed stacked against me, so I reassured myself that I was in exactly the right place. *I was going for it.* And as I readied myself for what would be a hectic, gruelling year, I broke down the potentially overwhelming concept of Selection into bite-sized chunks. I deconstructed the course into its component parts before breaking them down again into more manageable time-scales of weeks and days. By the time I'd arrived in the Brecon Beacons in Wales for the first assessment phase I had a simple psychological routine to lean into:

STEP ONE

Question: 'What do I need to do today?'
Answer: Eat, hydrate, pack my kit… And then work my arse off.

STEP TWO

Rinse and repeat. Day after day. *Get it done.*

There were moments where I would have been forgiven for buckling. During a particularly grim episode I picked up a stomach bug. God knows where it had started, but given the students were living at very close quarters it quickly ripped around the camp. I spent a full day vomiting and shitting through the eye of a needle, but I still forced myself over a series of hills during an infamous event on the Brecon Beacons known as Gilbert's Gut-Buster. The name was pretty apt. We were thrashed all day with a series of intense fireman's carries. Given my first act of the morning had been a mad dash to the khazi, I knew I was in for a rough ride, but when a number of other students raised their hands and voluntarily withdrew through illness, I felt strangely encouraged.

Not that the experience was made any less horrific. Even the Directing Staff could tell I was struggling. Up until that point I'd been physically strong and for much of the course I'd led the way on a number of timed marches. But I visibly faded as Gilbert's Gut-Buster began to build up. One of the Directing Staff even ran up to me to check on my condition.

'Stazicker, are you all right?' he said. 'There's no colour in your face.'

I shook my head. 'No, Staff, I don't feel too great. I've got the shits, but I'll crack on, until you tell me I can't or my body breaks down...'

The DS nodded. 'Yeah, roger. Just dig in.'

The pain didn't let up. I felt faint. My stomach cramped. At one point I was ordered to carry a six-foot-three bloke across my shoulders along a hilly trail. He must have weighed 100 kilos and my mind went into a spin.

Fucking hell! My world's imploding here, but if I can just put one foot in front of the other I might get through it...

I then tried to reframe the situation with some positive thought.

Wow, what an opportunity I have here. I'm on Selection. This is where I want to be right now...

I even tried to appreciate the rolling hills of South Wales.

What a beautiful place...

And just as I was finding some momentum, another member of the DS lurched in front of me. It was time for a verbal thrashing.

'Is that all you've got?' he said. 'It's fucking pathetic.'

The abuse went on for ages. He clearly wanted to break me. And then I watched as the instructor I'd spoken to previously pulled him to one side.

'Look, the man's got the shits, he's not loafing or taking his foot off the gas. He's actually digging out blind.'

The pressure eased up. Somehow I made it through the day, though it would take me another twenty-four hours before I felt vaguely human again. This, I told myself, was all part of being on Selection. In the build-up I'd understood that there would be many moments of excruciating discomfort and all I could do in those circumstances was push on, or quit – but there was no chance of me quitting. For my final assessment on the Brecon Beacons, I had to complete a march where anyone that failed to cross the line in the given time was immediately binned. Annoyingly, I'd rolled my ankle during a march the day previously. The joint had swollen up like a balloon and I was in agony. Rather than grumbling, I strapped it up as best I could and necked a load of strong painkillers.

The march itself was a war of attrition. Just putting one foot in front of the other felt like a Herculean effort and I was in so much pain, and dosed up with so many painkillers, that I started to hallucinate. At times it was possible to pick out one or two pink elephants along the horizon, but I rode out the suffering and crossed the finishing post in time. That night I had probably the best night's sleep of my life. I sunk a pint of Guinness to celebrate the fact that I'd somehow finished the first phase of Selection before falling into my bunk. When I woke around twelve hours later, there was only one question on my mind.

Have I done enough?

* * *

It's easy to think of significantly negative events as insurmountable setbacks, or disasters with the potential to alter our lives forever. Yes, some of them unquestionably are, especially those that involve personal tragedy, or a devastating physical or mental injury. However, with a change in attitude, it's possible to reconsider them as hugely valuable lessons. For example: grief teaches us about the temporary nature of time and the value of those people around us; an unexpected job loss can show us how to handle moments of financial turbulence; and a failed relationship might reveal a way of communicating more effectively and honestly with the people we share our lives with. All of these horrible events, while undoubtedly painful in the moment, can make us stronger if redefined.

My life was evidence of that. The death of my mum had been an emotional depth charge. Walking a tightrope of violence every afternoon on the way home from school made me feel vulnerable, scared and angry. Watching my football career disappear seemed like a massive setback. But I didn't let those events overwhelm me, or define my life in any way. Instead I turned them into narratives of strength, stories that told me I could both survive and achieve in challenging circumstances, whether that was in life, war or business. I've since been divorced. I've seen friends die in battle. I've made painful cock-ups during my ThruDark career. Yet, I'm still moving forward.

Don't get me wrong. I'm not for one second saying that this was an easy process. *It wasn't.* In fact all of those challenges felt horrendous back then, and the grief associated with losing a parent or friend doesn't get any smaller with time. I simply adapted as I became stronger and wiser. The same could be said of any personal errors I've made. Sadly, not everyone is able to learn from the mistakes in their life, or draw wisdom from negative events. For example, I've heard from many ex-military elite operatives, mates from the squadron, that the *real world* attitude towards work could be frustrating for them at times and when embarking upon new projects, endeavours or challenges, they fumed when the people around them – individuals without military experience that hadn't learned from adversity – failed to deliver. These new colleagues promised much without ever honouring their commitments. They were individuals that covered up their blunders and hid behind their flaws. And they rarely learned from their mistakes. As a result, complacency, ill discipline and poor decision-making caused great ideas to crash and burn. This was so different to my mates' previous experiences, where individuals with bad attitudes were binned off.

Both Louis and I were determined that this wouldn't happen with ThruDark. The elite military approach was everything when building our concept because we were forever being tripped up in the early stages and we understood that moaning or backing away from our disasters wouldn't help us. Rather than moaning or attempting to style out the latest novice error or setback, we 'fessed up to a mistake, assessed the path that had led us there, and then worked out the best ways in which to improve. Sometimes we even called in for reinforcements. From there, an understanding of how to grow pushed us on at an even faster rate.

As our work progressed, the frustration we'd felt when screwing up seemed to fade into the distance. And having learned from those screw-ups, exciting opportunities soon loomed large on the horizon.

ACTION ON
Outthink Your Flaws

In the middle of an unfolding disaster, it can be difficult to see a way out, let alone imagine that whatever is happening to you could possibly be a benefit in any way. However, once the healing has begun, take some time to consider the following ideas:

1. *Don't let your errors define or defeat you – they're building blocks to greater strength.*
   All of us fuck up, and in a big way – it's part of being human. Ultimately though, it's not the actual mistake that defines us, it's how we rebound. During Selection, the DS would hide in the foliage and make comments about a student's performance, or kit maintenance. Sometimes, there wasn't even an issue. They wanted to see if an exhausted, near broken, dehydrated individual would learn from the criticism, or wilt in the heat. Those that thrived were ranked highly. Those that crumbled were marked down. The elite wanted individuals that could grow from failure.

2. *Embrace your disasters, but only if you've learned from them – they're not an excuse.*
   It's easy to hide behind a traumatizing event, and many people will quit on a project, commitment or job because an unpleasant experience has caused them to doubt whether they're up to the task. I know. I've nearly died on

multiple occasions – in training too, not in the thick of a scrap – and my parachute incident is one such example. But quitting afterwards would have been the worst thing to do due to the fact that a) I'd have lost my prestigious position in the military, and b) I'd have wasted an educational lesson in staying calm under extreme pressure. That one accident became something I leaned into whenever the drama around me increased. It told me I could survive the worst case scenario.

3. *Learn to accept your weaknesses – either work to neutralize them, or delegate.*
   One of the key aspects of elite military service was self-awareness, which is why the egotist rarely thrived in our world. Those character types were often unable to understand their weak spots and as a result they struggled to improve upon them. Meanwhile, units were divided into small teams and the individuals within those teams carried certain specialities, all of them appropriate for the job in hand. Case point: I'd been trained as a sniper, so it was no good me stepping in first when a teammate had been shot. That was the patrol medic's job. You can do the same. Accept the flaws in your game. If you can't work to neutralize them, delegate to someone who specializes in that particular area whenever you're being exposed.

DEBRIEF

- All of us experience disaster in our lives from time to time. The trick is not to wear these events around our necks like badges of dishonour. Instead use them as lessons. *How can you improve from your mistakes?*

- You are not alone. Seriously: show me the person who doesn't know the sting of defeat, or claims not to have feelings of regret, and I'll show you a liar.

- In moments where extreme psychological pain threatens to kick you in, take your mind for a wander. In Selection, I imagined building a house from scratch. You might want to run through your favourite city, or go for a long motorbike ride in your head. See it in detail.

- Overcome imposter syndrome by reminding yourself of past achievements. Use them as fuel to drive you past any doubts you might have.

3

DARTS AT THE DARTBOARD

When planning product launches and new projects, Louis and I will repeat a mantra that's kept us steady since the inception of ThruDark – 'It's time to throw darts at the dartboard.' Or, in other words, 'Let's kick around some ideas and see if any hit the bullseye…' We'll consider good ones and bad ones; suggestions that might seem outrageous at first (but with a little tinkering could develop into a more tangible concept), and plans better suited to other issues within the business.

On the face of it, this process closely resembles a standard brainstorming session, but when working through it, we've retained two very important rules from our time in the military.

1. Nothing is judged, and nobody is rinsed if they're horribly wide of the mark on something.
2. The throwing doesn't end until the bullseye has been struck, because to put down the darts means admitting defeat.
   So far, this attitude has left us in pretty good shape.

Sticking to these two rules can be a challenging commitment, though. Persistence is required, resilience too, and I've noticed that many people can be quick to quit a project when their targets aren't landed immediately. However, the key to long-term success is to persevere, because once the bullseye has been hit, the hard work required for getting there – the sore arm, the endless days and weeks of practice – is quickly forgotten. Suddenly, you'll feel like an overnight success...

Throughout my military career I was constantly instructed to press ahead whenever missions went wrong, and to think outside the box in order to achieve results. The mentality was first instilled during the latter stages of Selection, where creative thinking and collective decision-making were considered valuable skills. However, once inserted into the theatre of combat, I witnessed how the concept of *throwing darts at the dartboard* could work equally well in life-or-death events.

When stepping into the idea of throwing darts at the dartboard, I've found it helps to think of the different elements of the game this way: the board is your mission, the arrows are your ideas, and landing the bullseye represents the optimum result, or best solution under the circumstances. Additionally, there are a couple of things I consider when preparing to throw darts with the ThruDark team. The first is a detail that sets the military elite's brainstorming sessions apart: when mission planning or working through a debrief, no operator's opinions are valued more highly because of their position or experience. Everyone is considered equal and the person with the least experience is as valuable as the most battle-tested because they have it in them to spot a detail, or notice something a senior officer might have missed.

This was a very different attitude to the one displayed within corporate culture, where the most powerful voices, or those with the most experience, hold the biggest influence. (In some businesses there is even an acronym for this very situation: HIPPO, or the Highest Paid Person's Opinion.) The downside of these set-ups is that age, rank and image often come to trump genuine innovation and great ideas die on the vine because they've been presented by an individual outside the senior leadership, or a younger, greener member of the team. This was something we were very keen to avoid at ThruDark, and as the company expanded and extra employees came on board, we've considered the opinions of the newest members of the team as much as the most experienced. Everyone is on an equal footing because we understand that all of us are capable of suggesting an idea that might change the game in the planning phases of a new product launch, or as we're reacting to a supply issue or design challenge.

The second important detail concerns the stripping away of emotions when it comes to decision-making. It's often the case that the *optimum* dart might not be the *perfect* outcome, but if it's the most suitable under the circumstances then it pays to commit to that decision or idea, all the while dialling down any negative feelings you or the group might be experiencing. I know this moment all too well because I've lived it, having previously decided to sell my military medals in order to financially contribute towards the early formation of the company. This might sound like a controversial dart to throw for those of you that have served with the military, but when the decision was made I'd been struggling through a difficult divorce with my now ex-wife. I was also in the final stages of leaving the military and working out how to fund the business with Louis. There were many sleepless nights. It felt at times as if I was spinning too many plates and I feared the whole lot could come crashing down at any moment. Matters eventually came to a head when I was told that my medals were going to be sucked into the financial settlement of the divorce, in much the same way that a piece of art or some other asset would.

'Fucking hell,' I thought. 'Even if I don't sell these medals, I'm going to get financially hammered for simply owning them.'

I looked into the finances and what I could expect to receive in an auction. Having realized that the money was going to establish a financial future for my ex and our eldest son, Lucas – which they absolutely deserved – while leaving a little surplus cash for the business, I decided it was the right decision to make. *Was it an easy one?* Of course not. The medals were representative of one or two major milestones in my military career and I was extremely proud of them. But when I really thought about it, those achievements weren't being sold, nor were my medals being stripped from me. They were simply a physical representation of my past successes and I still had psychological ownership of those. In their purest form they were pieces of metal and fabric, and as we all know, drowning sailors don't hold on to gold bars.

Having thrown my darts and landed at the best possible decision, it was important to accept the outcome without moaning. In the end, those medals ushered in a new era of freedom. With our combined funds, Louis and I were in a position to execute our early business plans and the money was invested in materials, designs, accountants and PR. At that time I believed it was the right move for me personally. *I still do*. Whether I'll feel the same way in thirty years' time, I'm not sure, but at the moment I feel OK about it – selling was the best solution in what was becoming an insurmountable problem. The truth is that all of us will have difficult choices to make throughout our lives, especially when our feet are being held to the fire. That was mine.

The lesson learned? Accept the solutions when they arrive and move forward with purpose.

And never complain.

ACTION ON
Take Charge of the Dartboard

Throwing darts at the dartboard is a game and there are ways of tweaking the concept, or altering the rules to suit your situation:

1. Change the target.
   No professional darts player would attempt to hit a bullseye from 100 feet, so your ideas should be realistic and within reach. When creating ThruDark, the aim of becoming one of the biggest technical clothing brands on the planet was never suggested. We wanted to be a powerful presence in a competitive market. Likewise, when trying to extract our injured teammate from the aforementioned ambush, nobody volunteered a ballsy idea that was 100 per cent guaranteed to end in multiple deaths. We planned rationally instead. These boundaries also hold true for any planning phase: be ambitious, but rational. Don't throw your darts from a million miles away.

2. Enjoy the game.
   Sometimes decision-making happens under extreme pressure. When ThruDark started, there were limited investment funds to play with, and so we were more selective in our dart throwing, but we remained resolute. The key to this perseverance was to make the process fun. Our friendship and the fact we both enjoyed working

THE HARD ROAD WILL TAKE YOU HOME

together really helped and at no time did anyone feel as if a gun was being held to their heads. Your dart-throwing sessions can take on the same approach. Suggestions:

○ Leave the office and visit a space where people feel relaxed and can kick around ideas.
○ Make the most of those post-workout endorphins and get creative after a period of collective exercise.
○ Go to the pub and step up to the oche with a pint. With collective willpower, you'll soon land the optimal dart.

3. The golden shot won't happen straightaway.
   By all means think big when throwing your darts, but don't become disheartened if the perfect solution doesn't present itself with the first throw. Unicorn companies like Apple or Amazon didn't happen overnight, they took a hell of a lot of work. Teams that overcome threatening issues rarely solve them instantaneously and it's just as likely your challenge will be the same. When planning under pressure in Selection, I felt as if I was constantly adjusting my aim and missing the target. I became physically and mentally exhausted, but I never quit because I was passionate about the end result and I usually arrived at a suitable solution. The lads who made it through were those that kept throwing darts, unless instructed otherwise by the DS.

DEBRIEF

♦ In moments of pressure, throw darts at the dartboard. Get your team together and keep lobbing ideas around until an optimum result is achieved.

♦ Forget the hierarchy. Imagine the possibilities if a company or project accepted the opinions of everyone within its structure from time to time, regardless of age, rank, experience and time served.

♦ When your optimum dart has landed, accept the result, even though what you have to do might be painful or emotionally uncomfortable in some way.

4

RED CELL ANALYSIS

All of us have weaknesses, either individually or as part of a larger group. It's one of the reasons why so many professional sports teams have an army of scouts at their disposal. These analysts are paid to study the opposition in the hope that their technical insights will expose a series of flaws that can be exploited in a forthcoming fixture. But studies of this kind are also effective when the spotlight is turned inwards, especially in business when it's important that a company self-improves in order to stay ahead of their nearest rivals and away from market disruption.

This type of analysis is very popular in the military where we tend to self-assess to the nth degree; it's not uncommon for our tactics and procedures to be scrutinized until the weakest links within them have been minimized. On a short-term level, this is most evident in technology and the weapons systems used on the ground – they're constantly being updated. On a long-term level, attack timings and asset deployments are studied and adjusted according to factors such as geopolitics.

The overarching aim of these checks is to allow a fighting group to function at their optimum and, by extension, maintain a tactical superiority in the battlespace. Within a business setting, though, a similar mindset can prove just as effective...

At certain points during the development of ThruDark, our team has leant upon an assessment we call the Red Cell Analysis, a procedure in which we check for weaknesses in our operational set-up, such as production methods, distribution and even security. It's worth noting that the work doesn't stop once a Red Cell Analysis has been conducted. The team will constantly assess and reassess the situation, changing their set-up if required. This might sound like quite an extreme practice to apply to a business setting, but wealthy companies with highly valuable intellectual property have run similarly exhaustive safety checks. On one occasion, Louis and I – plus one or two other former elite operators – were even invited by a tech company to stress-test the security systems in place at their HQ after they'd decided to check their facility was secure from invaders, burglars and other external threats.

'We're pretty confident in our security systems,' they said. 'Do your worst.'

So we did. We didn't have to try very hard, either.

Our first step was to purchase suits and go undercover as businessmen, the type of people that might have been employed at a nearby company. From there, we staked out the building at various times of the day in order to gather intelligence on its security profile – who was coming and going, and where and when. We hung out in nearby cafes and bars, and eavesdropped on people we suspected to be employees. We then followed those same staff members home and became familiar with their names and faces; if anyone logged into the shared Wi-Fi of a local coffee shop or bar, it became pretty easy to hack into their laptops. Having scooped all sorts of personal details – names, company positions, addresses and so on – we were able to create a handful of fake company IDs. By the time our infiltration hour had arrived, we'd secured as much security clearance as any member of the team.

Accessing the offices was then fairly straightforward. Thanks to our comprehensive surveillance we knew the ins and outs of the company's security infrastructure. On the day, Louis and I entered the building in the type of work clothes worn by the company's staff members. We walked through the foyer confidently, as if our arrival was an everyday event, and cruised through the first layer of protection with our fake IDs. Others accessed the property via a side door, a location we'd recognized as somewhere the smokers tended to congregate during the day. By mixing in with the crowd, making small talk and then subtly jamming the door when everybody had returned to their desks, it was possible to breach the building's external defences. *All of us were now inside.*

When we showed our results to the company, they were horrified.

Red Cell Analysis-style procedures have become increasingly popular in big business. For example, high-profile online companies often entice hackers to force their way into their databases, usually with cash incentives. Sometimes, resourceful individuals are even rewarded with a lucrative position on the company's online security team. (Because it's always far better to have someone inside the tent, pissing out, than someone outside, pissing in.) At ThruDark we've run through the Red Cell Analysis in two ways. The first was structural: we've checked and enhanced the security systems at our company HQ and added layers of security around the pricey stock and equipment stored there. The second was an intellectual analysis, where we assessed our working practices, tactics and targets. I'll talk you through both procedures now.

RED CELL ANALYSIS No. 1
Structural Safety

When the company first established our HQ down in Poole, we went crazy, up-armouring *everything*. Cameras scoured every inch of the property and a series of sensors pinged out alerts to our phones if any uninvited guests approached the perimeter. Every door was fixed with double bolts, while barriers were positioned in front of the building to prevent our rolling shutters from being rammed during a smash-and-grab raid. When our insurance company arrived to assess the premises, they couldn't believe the effort we'd put into securing the place.

'Bloody hell,' said the rep. 'You couldn't have actually done any more… Other than putting bars on the upper windows.'

I felt too embarrassed to tell him that we'd considered doing exactly that. (We'd only held off after realizing it would have created a prison cell vibe.)

So far, the set-up has proved effective and the property hasn't yet been breached, though a neighbouring business was broken into during a night burglary. Luckily, the crew failed to get away with anything because *our* surveillance systems had picked them up and we alerted the police who showed up to arrest them five minutes later.

In a side note, it's always worth running a Red Cell Analysis on your personal security systems at home, especially if you're storing or moving valuable assets. For example, we're at our most vulnerable when sitting down in our cars. We mess about with keys, the stereo and seat belts without thinking to lock the doors.

This is the moment when most carjackers usually strike. I'm even cautious when I *leave* the car. When I pull up on my drive, I'll take a look around. *Does everything appear OK? Are the security lights on? Is anyone home?*

Elsewhere, I've up-armoured my house by adding various layers of security. I have pre-sensor tech in my doorway, the doors are double locked and double bolted, and there are surveillance cameras all over the property. There's even a panic button inside the house for my wife to use if anyone tries to break in. Meanwhile, I practise situational awareness whenever I'm on the move and I'll check my position and the position of any other people around me when I'm walking about. These are old habits from my military days dying hard, I know. But one thing I've learned is that everyone assumes the worst-case scenario will never impact upon them – until the moment when it actually does.

RED CELL ANALYSIS No. 2
Procedural Safety

Aside from our Fort Knox levels of security, we've taken a series of steps to bombproof our financial momentum whenever the company has taken a leap forward. That might sound strange – after all, growth is a good thing and should be regarded as a moment of excitement. But sometimes a fighting force can be at their most vulnerable following on from victory, especially if they've taken their eye off the target. Likewise growth can leave a company or individual exposed to new challenges and unfamiliar risks. To counteract those threats we made sure to check our financials and infrastructure with every forward step. Then we asked ourselves a series of challenging questions regarding potential areas of development.

Examples:
1. *Will we leave ourselves exposed by massively expanding the ThruDark workforce?*
2. *Are we missing a trick by not having a bricks-and-mortar store?*
3. *Could we rely on online sales only when our expanding target audience is notoriously reluctant to engage with the returns process?*

The answers, when we eventually landed upon them, were reassuring and set the tone for the business going forward. They were as follows:

1. In terms of personnel expansion we decided it was important to remain dynamic. Larger businesses and big brands move like cruise liners: it takes them forever to change course, thanks to their multi-level chains of command and complex communications systems. Louis and I decided it was vital that ThruDark remained adaptable in order to change pace and direction at any given moment, which proved highly effective when the pandemic kicked off in 2020 and the world was plunged into lockdown.

2. Given how the world changed during that time, the debate surrounding a bricks-and-mortar store was much easier to answer: it suddenly made even more sense for ThruDark to remain as an online presence only, rather than building out a physical flagship premises. Given everybody had been forced to temporarily operate through e-commerce, the decision eventually proved a shrewd one as we'd already upped our presence on social media platforms such as Instagram and Facebook. Our main concern at that point was fairly basic: *how can we make the buying process easier?* We realized very quickly that while it was beyond us to operate like a Nike-style retail monster, ThruDark had the potential to attract attention on a highly credible level, and we posted shots of our ambassadors such as Jason Fox or Victoria Pendleton wearing the latest product drops. This drove potential customers to the website which then translated into sales.

3. The final question of our target audience's shopping habits was, admittedly, a bit of a head-scratcher. Blokes made up a large chunk of our customer base (though we do have lines for both men and women) and were notoriously fickle when it came to online buying. A lot of men admitted to being annoyed by the returns process and they tended to purchase items that they knew would fit them and suited their look, rather than trying out ten styles and returning nine. I'd always preferred to try things on in a store, especially big-ticket brands. It helped me to run through the basic details of what I was splashing out on: the fit, the feel; *does it look cool?* With those vital details checked off, I'd be more likely to make the purchase.

Meanwhile, the thought of buying stuff online and then hauling several parcels to the post office a few days later (having printed out the return labels) didn't appeal to me. At ThruDark we decided our best response was to make the returns process as simple as possible. We placed a label into the packaging along with a note explaining that the process was free. No cost, no drama.

With our vulnerable points identified and assessed through a Red Cell Analysis, we were then able to press ahead with confidence at a time when some companies might have caved under the pressure of a global pandemic.

ACTION ON
Bulletproof Your Successes

When things are running smoothly, it's easy to view the Red Cell Analysis as a pain in the arse. Or to think, 'We're in good shape. The business is bulletproof.' But some entities that were once considered too big to fail have famously been exposed – and in fairly painful fashion. Leaders become complacent, empires collapse, and there are some pretty notable examples of previously market-topping companies that were challenged unexpectedly by disruptive technologies and industry newcomers. Having failed to identify their weak spots, they were later outfought and out-thought in the battle.

One high-profile example was the film rental company Blockbuster, who disappeared from view having first been challenged by the then DVD postal service, Netflix, and its rival, LoveFilm. They were then crushed when Netflix became an online streaming service. It is 20/20 hindsight I know, but had Blockbuster taken a longer look at the emerging technologies in their field and the disruptive companies building momentum around them, there's every chance they might have found the time to expand their business model and avoid disaster.

This is where the Red Cell Analysis makes for a handy tool: it acts as an early warning alarm system for those moments when trouble might be developing around us unseen. How we actually implement that alarm system varies upon the circum-stances in which we're operating, but if you're looking for pointers, try the following:

Personnel: *Are your staff/co-workers feeling satisfied or dissatisfied? Is there a chance you might lose a key team member to a rival entity? Is there a player in the market that might be worth sounding out for future employment?*

Finances: *Are you fiscally solid for the next three, six and twelve months? What about five years? A common mistake newly self-employed people make is to assume they'll be paid on time – is there a buffer fund in the bank for the opening six months?*

Outside forces: *Are you able to function during an unforeseen disaster, such as a supply chain issue, or a government lockdown? Are you keeping an eye on the disruptive tech in your field? Are there any legislative requirements coming down the track that might affect you in the future, such as the carbon footprint of your business?*

By answering these questions, we can fix any breaches in our armour, while planning a strategy for any troublesome events, should they occur in the future.

DEBRIEF

◆ What would happen if I were to run a Red Cell Analysis on your finances or business? *Would you survive the intense scrutiny?* Work to locate your weak spots and correct them.

◆ Fix your structural security by running a Red Cell Analysis on your home or office. Just how easy would it be for someone to compromise the property and wreak havoc?

◆ It's worth checking your online security by regularly changing your passwords. Invest in security software and a Virtual Private Network (VPN), which protects your identity across the internet.

5

HOW YOU DO ANYTHING IS HOW YOU DO *EVERYTHING*

A common misconception about the elite operator is that we're super soldiers: freaks of nature, stronger, faster, tougher and smarter than the rest. And sure, one or two elements of this statement definitely ring true. We've been battle-hardened in such a way that it's possible to thrive in chaotic extremes more readily than other wings of the military, but really the fundamentals of our skills and successes are fairly boring: we plan meticulously and perform with an intense diligence in everything we do. It's the special sauce that guarantees expert performance.

How does this work? Well, on a bigger picture level, our missions are planned in meticulous detail. When a job kicks off for real, everyone involved understands what's required and what they're expected to do in order to achieve mission success. But in the short term, an operator will clean their weapon fastidiously. They'll take care of their kit and check and then double-check their equipment before every battle. Nobody wants a technical balls-up in the thick of a gunfight.

That attitude has been brought across to ThruDark. Whenever I've swept the warehouse floor, I haven't rested until everything has been left spotless. The same attention goes into product planning, sales meetings, and picking and packing – a process in which we post our online orders. Not everyone thinks this way, though. People can be lazy. As a society, we don't even have to leave our sofas to receive a meal. We can just tap our phones and a takeaway magically appears. However, by embracing discipline and control, and ignoring the temptations of convenience, or laziness, it's possible to bring tangible improvements to our daily lives...

Let me give you an example of how badly things can go wrong when you *don't* follow the principle of 'How you do anything is how you do *everything*...'

My unit had endured a busy night. The work was intense. We'd been running around with our heads on fire for hours, but as I sprinted towards a target in the dark, an important piece of equipment failed. *Shit!* The batteries had died. For a few moments I felt exposed and unable to function properly.

Instantly I took a knee and fumbled around in my belt for the spares I always kept with me, my brain racing at the consequences of a technical failure. *What if the lads started shooting without me? What if I missed an enemy gunman in the immediate area?* Then I remembered how I'd got myself into such a state in the first place. During the previous evening there wasn't a lot of action, and when we'd returned to base I hadn't bothered to change the batteries in my hardware.

'It'll be all right,' I'd told myself. 'These things last for fifteen, sixteen hours. I've got enough charge.'

Not twenty-four hours later, that lazy lapse in judgement had bitten me on the arse.

'Fuck!' I thought, sliding the new batteries into place. 'What if this had happened while I'd been running into a room? *Or if someone had needed me to take a shot?*'

I vowed to never take the lazy option again.

There was no real need to massively reassess my processes in the aftermath, however. I wasn't one to cut corners ordinarily; this mistake was very much out of character, and I'd been trained to be a kit care pest from the second I'd joined with the Royal Marines Commandos when, as part of our basic training, the importance of uniform maintenance had been drummed into us on the parade ground. The lads were forever being ordered to shine their boots and present their kit perfectly and anyone unable to reach the required standards was physically punished with a series of push-ups, or a lengthy commando crawl up and down the nearest muddy hill. That always acted as a stern motivator. This same level of detail was also applied to housekeeping in the barracks and at times I felt like a professional cleaner.

'Why the fuck am I being asked to do this?' I'd think as I pressed the cuffs and collars of my shirts, and scrubbed the toilets.

In reality I was being psychologically primed for a series of ideas that were much bigger in scale. In many ways, the process echoed a theme from *The Karate Kid* – that famous martial arts movie from the 1980s. In a well-known scene, the student, Daniel LaRusso, is instructed to complete a series of menial chores by his *sensei*, Mr Miyagi. He's told to sand the floors and paint a series of fence panels. At one point, Daniel is even tasked with cleaning the vintage cars in Mr Miyagi's forecourt. Daniel's frustration soon boils over, but when he then throws a strop, the technical movements in those mind-numbing tasks are revealed to be physical building blocks for a series of highly effective karate moves. In much the same way, and without us really knowing it, the boring duties dumped upon us throughout basic training were instilling a higher level of discipline and attention to detail in *everything* we did. Those traits would prove vitally important when it later came to the technical aspects of weapon maintenance, combat survival and mission planning.

It wasn't just the military that installed practices of this kind. Similar levels of attentiveness go into the multi-million pound businesses of sport, and in Formula One, a pit-stop team will practise small, individual movements over and over, on and off the track, in order to shave a fraction of a second from the tricky process of tyre changes. Everyone has to be on point and alert for a pit stop to succeed and if one person misses their cue, or forgets a vital piece of kit as the car approaches, a three-second pit procedure can quite easily become a twenty-second nightmare. There's really no room for shit discipline.

In order to improve my own personal performance I've established a few psychological pointers, reminders that are easily applied to my daily processes in business, home life and play. Many of them have been born of military service, where phrases such as 'the relentless pursuit of excellence', or 'in union there's strength' were drummed into me during training and Selection. Those same phrases were later recalled in combat, where they helped to steady me during pressurized events. Away from war, though, a handful of cues always spring to mind whenever I'm looking to maintain focus or if I want to execute a task diligently…

1. DO THE RIGHT THING WHEN NO ONE'S LOOKING

It's very easy to skip over an action, or to ignore a problem if we're alone, or working solo. The messy workstation, that jammed printer or an overflowing recycling bin are easily breezed past if our colleagues or loved ones aren't around to see them. There's a temptation to think: 'Well, if I don't deal with that, nobody will know.' Or, on the reverse: 'If I *do* sort it, no one's paying attention and I won't get the credit.' The difference between the elite operator and the regular soldier – or the average business person and the market dominating leader for that matter – is that they'll perform those annoying tasks to the best of their ability, even if no one's around to praise them.

Those hardware batteries aside, I was a stickler when it came to military routine, as was everybody around me. Regardless of whether my squadron commanders or team leaders were looking, I'd perform a series of housekeeping duties after each and every mission, and in the following order:

a) I'd clean my weapon attentively, because to give it a quick wipe down was a dangerous oversight. Nobody wanted to enter into a serious gunfight only for a round to jam. 'Why didn't I clean my weapons system properly?' is a set of famous last words no operator would want on their tombstone.

b) Equipment check. I'd assess the kit that helped to keep me alive on the job, such as my radio and optics. Any problems or shortfalls would be rectified immediately. (As I explained earlier, this lesson was learned the hard way.)

c) Finally, I'd take care of myself by eating, showering and then resting for as long as possible before the next operation. It's worth noting that between moments of action, an operator was expected to maintain peak physical fitness. For the most part, the job kept us sharp. Running out of helicopters or walking on to targets while lugging heavy kit and weaponry made for gruelling work. But on those very rare, very quiet days, I'd make sure to work out at the base. I didn't want my body to fail when I needed it most.

Small habits of this kind build discipline. It's why successful business minds are forever telling us to make our beds in the morning – *and they're right*. Introducing one or two routines that can be performed to a consistently high standard (while no one's looking) is a great way of instilling self-mastery without having to drastically rewire your life. However, while tiny habits can lead to big results, those results can be both good and bad – depending on the habit – so the trick is to pack the day with positive actions. Don't wolf a bowl of sugary cereal down while you wait for the kettle to boil at breakfast – stretch or do some push-ups and squats instead. Deal with your hardest work tasks when you start the working day and square away your desk at the end of the shift. Sort your kit and clothes for the next morning before going to bed rather than leaving it to the last minute. Maybe read ten pages of a book before turning off the lights instead of scrolling through social media. Oh, and always take the stairs instead of the lift. The positive actions you choose are irrelevant really, the important thing is to execute every one to the best of your ability. A sense of diligence will soon creep into everything you do as a result, especially if you're the only one around to appreciate the effort.

2. THE SEVEN Ps

Military training is full of mnemonics – phrases or acronyms used to assist the memory, or to remind an individual of a certain operating system – at every level. One that helped me throughout active service focused on 'The Seven Ps', which, when picked apart, informed an operator that '*Prior planning and preparation prevents piss-poor performance*'. This cue has since helped ThruDark as we've found our footing within a highly competitive market, and nowadays Louis and I will recall it before every stage in our development, whether that's been the launch of a new clothing range, the production of kit for a specialist event (such as Nimsdai Purja's historical climb on K2 during the winter of 2021) or a website redesign. We prep and we plan, hoping to avoid an aborted launch, a fatal kit failure or a below-par website.

This process hasn't been confined to one-off events, either. When it comes to the day-to-day running of the company, the team will study every aspect of the business from top to bottom with the view that there's always room to improve, tweak or grow. During product design sessions, we'll constantly analyse zips, buttons and pockets to see if we can deliver more functionality. The website will be checked and double-checked for user experience and authenticity. (For a while, we even replaced the arrow cursor with a weapon sight because it felt more in tune with our image.) Elsewhere, we're forever improving how we pick and pack our deliveries in order to run the sales and distribution department as efficiently as possible.

When things have gone wrong, either through our fault or the fault of others, we've taken control of the situation as quickly as possible. There have been times when a product sample or a finished garment has arrived at the ThruDark HQ and it hasn't been quite right for one reason or another. The issue has sometimes been tiny, unnoticeable to most customers, but because of the Seven Ps we've felt duty-bound to resolve it. Rather than sending out the orders and crossing our fingers, hoping nobody notices, we've paused production and then explained the situation to our customers immediately. Because not preparing a launch properly, or covering up a mistake can be a fatal blow in a business where customer loyalty is everything.

3. LOVE MANY, TRUST FEW

Maybe you're a diligent person. Maybe you've got a positive routine in place and a thirst for self-improvement. That's great, but sadly not everyone feels the same way, and that's OK too. The truth is that we're all guilty of being lazy from time to time. I know I have in the past, and I might be in the future, but at no point have I claimed that perfecting the art of meticulous planning and diligent performance is a piece of piss. It takes time and effort, and I know that if I were to break down my life into days, weeks and months, I'd find one or two occasions where I've brushed over a detail, or dodged a task because I couldn't be arsed. Some of the time I might have got away with it; on other occasions I haven't, but it's those lapses that have proved most painful later on down the line. In the fallout, I've resolved to improve the situation as soon as possible.

When the backdraft to poor discipline lands upon you, and only you, there's always room to learn and grow. But in life, other people will let you down too, even the associates you've come to rely upon because they, like everyone else, *like you*, can suffer from the odd lapse in judgement. They want to cut corners. They want to make their day-to-day a little easier. *It's human nature.* Perhaps something horrendous has kicked off in their personal life and they're not able to think clearly. Maybe they're frazzled or overloaded. That's all fine if it only impacts upon their product or service. However, if it impacts upon *yours*, then real problems can emerge and I've learned at first hand not to trust other people's word.

For example, when scrapping in Afghanistan, my

vehicle patrol was ordered into the desert. As we departed I asked the driver, a local soldier, whether he'd checked the fuel tank.

'Yes,' he said, sounding pretty sure of himself.

'How much have we got?'

He raised a hand to show me the levels in the tank. 'I'm happy,' he said. Again, he seemed pretty confident.

Typically, we broke down just a couple of hours later. *The vehicle had run out of fuel within spitting distance of the forward operating base we were heading towards.* After that screw-up, I made a point of checking the fuel personally before setting out on a patrol. I didn't want to be let down again.

When it comes to running a business, or starting a new project, it's important to surround yourself with the people you trust implicitly. I'm currently writing this chapter from the office at ThruDark. I can see the other lads buzzing around in the warehouse, putting in a shift, sorting orders diligently and picking and packing. I know all of them are of the same mindset as Louis and me: *They want the brand to succeed.* Really, that's the key to success. If the team around you is pulling in the right direction, and working with discipline and with an attention to detail, you're on the right course. If the collective have become mentally bogged down by slack behaviour and lazy thinking, then trouble is just around the corner. Make sure to pick your allies carefully.

4. DON'T LET GREAT IDEAS KILL COMMON SENSE

Everyone enduring Selection is assessed on clarity of thinking as much as physical resilience and the military elite requires schemers and operators who can improvise under pressure. More importantly, they're not overly keen on mavericks, extreme risk-takers, hotheads or eccentrics – character types that can be moulded in the regular army, but in the top tier cause more harm than good. That's not to say we can't get carried away from time to time and I've watched as experienced personnel have become distracted by what has appeared like an ingenious idea on paper, only for it to fall apart under scrutiny. As far as I'm concerned, the golden rule is this: as with free lunches and get-rich-quick schemes, if a plan looks too good to be true, it usually is.

One story that illustrates this concept took place when I was working in the UK in a role that required me to mission plan alongside the type of geeky scientists that you might expect to find in a basement workshop during a James Bond film. Their job was to design equipment that would push the boundaries of what was possible in the theatre of war; they were allowed to create without limits. Mine was to test new inventions; I understood what worked and what didn't within a battle space. One day, after testing out some fancy new portable equipment, everything seemed to be running smoothly. Then one operator raised his hand.

'So how are we supposed to stick this stuff down?' he said. 'There's no attachments or strapping...'

One by one, the tech department started mumbling and

looking at one another. 'Well... Er... *We don't know.*'

We couldn't believe it. For all their undoubted ingenuity in creating what was a really useful piece of kit, the basic principles within their design had been overlooked. Eventually, their team leader turned to us and shrugged his shoulders.

'Er, what do you think? Any ideas?'

For ten minutes we threw out suggestions that included the addition of adjustable Velcro attachments and even magnets. When a solution was settled upon, the same team leader scolded his unit.

'Why didn't you think of that?'

This was all a bit of a giggle while we'd been training, but had this design flaw not been identified, there's every chance a disaster would have taken place when the equipment was used for real. It was for this reason that Louis and I realized we would have to apply the same common sense attitude in business as we had in service. Sure, there would be every chance for us to flex our creative muscles and then push the boundaries of what was expected in an Arctic parka or summit suit, but at the same time those products had to actually work. As a result we dreamed large and pushed ourselves technologically without ever drifting too far into a fantasy world where water pouches were built into mountain coats (a bad idea all round) and heating pads were fixed to heavy-duty trousers (ludicrously expensive).

We've also decided to surround ourselves with subject matter experts from the relevant areas in our industry. We consult with successful business types, experienced designers and people we consider to be very experienced in the fields of textiles, production, logistics, marketing and finance. In fact, we've almost accidentally structured our associates in such a way that when it comes to arranging a brand strategy meeting, we're sometimes the least experienced people in the room. Likewise, if ever we attend conferences or seminars, we're often outgunned in terms of time in the job. While this might feel like an intimidating experience at first, it helps if these sessions are treated as intelligence-gathering exercises and a chance to learn. Both Louis and I have become very comfortable when admitting to being too green to grasp a concept or tactic. If ever a discussion has gone to another level and we're feeling lost, one of us will raise our hand and ask for a basic explanation. Every time we'll come away having grown in some way.

This same attitude served us well in the military. During elite service I found myself surrounded by experts, either in the group of operators I was fighting with, or instructors on Added Qualification (ADDQUAL) courses. When it came to working alongside team leaders and the squadron bosses, I would pick up new intelligence on geopolitics, or a style of tactical analysis I hadn't known about previously. Often I'd come away thinking, 'Bloody hell, I'd have never thought of that.' It wasn't always me that was asking the questions, either. All of the lads were encouraged to pipe up if there was something they didn't understand, because it was vital that everyone was aware of their roles and responsibilities before a mission. This created a learning environment where everyone benefited.

The same style of learning can work for you. Up-skill. Sign up for new courses. Fill your team with experts and experienced minds. And never be afraid to ask questions. I'm forever chipping in with queries during meetings. I approach work missions by gathering as much info as I can through reading, listening and watching – I have a genuine appetite for knowledge and I want to better myself. To become elite, you should take the same approach.

ACTION ON
Hope is Not a Plan

The ThruDark website undergoes a radical transformation from time to time. We add bells and whistles, various functions become increasingly user-friendly, and the home page is reworked and styled in such a way that it appears more in tune with the company's core values – honour, integrity, loyalty and trust. One issue that was out of my hands was the techy side of the job, and during the last redesign I remember checking in with one of the designers responsible for the overhaul. Our team had worked through a long list of improvements and I wanted to know whether everything was going to run smoothly upon launching. *Were we in good shape? Are we going to launch on time?*

'Yeah,' he said. *'Hopefully.'*

In any situation where one potential consequence of failure is fatal – whether that's physical, emotional, reputational or even financial – hope doesn't make for a reassuring safety net. A unit of operators wouldn't drop into a compound *hoping* to meet an underprepared enemy. They'd use the intelligence at their disposal to paint the clearest possible picture of what's happening on the ground. Likewise, a surgeon wouldn't open up a patient *hoping* they're not allergic to anaesthetics. They'd check their medical notes beforehand.

As far as I'm concerned, hope is not a plan, so ThruDark certainly wasn't going to launch a costly and valuable website redesign without checking the system for glitches and flaws. Instead, we took action, reassessing the situation by checking for any potential issues while bombproofing the design from front to back. The added workload was huge. It placed an extra strain on everyone. But the result was a product that the team was happy to launch and there was no need for large-scale maintenance work beyond its release.

My advice: *do not rely on hope*. Instead apply due diligence to everything you do. By doing so the bad habit of crossing your fingers and praying for the best will never come into play.

DEBRIEF

◆ Whenever faced with a necessary task, ask yourself a question: *Is anyone looking?* Then do it anyway.

◆ Adopt an elite attitude to upgrading your skills by taking on new courses and learning new disciplines, whether they're directly linked to your ambitions or not. They might help you in abstract ways. For example, a welding course might teach you about mindfulness; taking up indoor climbing will teach you how to plan under pressure.

◆ Always remember the Seven Ps. Write the mnemonic down and shove it in your kit bag. Stick it to your fridge. Say the phrase out loud when you're tempted to cut corners.

PART TWO

TECHNIQUES, TACTICS & PROCEDURES

BRIEFING

Passing Royal Marines Commandos basic training was one thing. Being inserted into the theatre of conflict was a whole other game altogether and nothing fully prepared me for the pressures of war. The discovering was in the doing though, and I quickly learned that in combat I could thrive in an environment where the issues of success and failure could be decided in a matter of split seconds, rather than minutes or hours.

My first ever tour of duty highlighted this reality. I was twenty-two years old, a still-wet-behind-the-ears kid and I had no idea of how I was going to react to my first IED, or moment of contact. Though I can clearly remember one of my first urban patrols in a war zone. I was part of a convoy of four or five 'snatch' vehicles and our wagon was positioned at the rear. I was standing in the back with another lad who was way more experienced than me and our role was to keep any civilian vehicles a good distance away from the convoy.

In those situations there was a very clear scale of escalation that determined how and when we should react. The first step was to point to a sign that stated 'Keep 20 Metres Away' – it had been written in the local language and was clearly visible from a distance. Anyone who came any nearer could expect to receive some aggressive posturing. This started with a warning shot and from there, if we'd been unable to make our presence felt, our next move was to fire a round into the engine block. If that didn't work (and we suspected the driver was a suicide bomber) it was within our rights to take a fatal shot.

Unsurprisingly, the locals didn't pay too much attention to the rules. Having grown accustomed to our presence they were happy to push the boundaries, especially as we were sometimes quite slow on the roads. It wasn't uncommon for a convoy to be buzzed by blokes on motorbikes or a frustrated driver. During this one patrol a car had appeared at our back and was closing in on us steadily. It was much nearer than the stipulated 20 metres and as I waved to the driver in an attempt to keep him back, the vehicle kept on coming. My teammate, who had probably witnessed what could go wrong in an environment where suicide bombings were becoming a regular event, seemed edgy.

'Fire a warning shot,' he yelled.

Rather than doing as he said, I held back. I felt confident. I was fully trained and though I'd not yet fired a round in anger, the techniques I'd picked up in training had taught me how to function.

The other soldier wasn't happy about my assessment. 'Fucking fire! Do a warning shot!'

I shook my head. 'I feel fine with the situation,' I said. 'If you feel we should shoot, you shoot.'

Thankfully the driver at our rear eased off the gas and faded into the distance, but who knows what would have happened if

I'd popped off a round? What I realized in that moment was that the techniques, tactics and procedures I'd picked up in training had been stepping stones and they'd kept me calm. I'd been able to make a level-headed decision in a stressful moment and later, when I served on more specialized and dangerous operations, the processes instilled in me by the military elite turned me into a highly functioning asset. I was able to think clearly when the shooting started; I learned to psychologically set myself in events that seemed to be spinning out of control and I discovered strategies that would help me to overcome a threatening enemy.

Meanwhile, the small units I served with were 'force multipliers'. We were able to appear much larger in numbers than we truly were, and when coming up against heavily-armed enemy groups we were able to turn our underdog status into an advantage. Most importantly, I was encouraged to learn new skills and self-improve in such a way that I became a versatile and flexible weapon. Though I was a tier one operator, it was important that I remained a constant work in progress.

I've since learned that these strategies and mindsets are just as applicable to any career or challenge. In many ways, they've driven me towards successes I probably couldn't have imagined as a twenty-two-year-old Marine, perched on the back of a snatch vehicle, a potential suicide bomber speeding towards me. The reality is this though: the rhythms of war and everyday life weirdly echo one another. There are moments of stillness and moments of anarchy; there are teachable lessons and opportunities for growth; and having the right techniques, tactics and procedures in place for each gives us a greater chance of succeeding…

6

KAIZEN

Stripped down to its core principles, Kaizen is the Japanese concept of continual improvement. When applied to business, Masaaki Imai – founder of the Kaizen Institute and author of Kaizen: The Key to Japan's Competitive Success *– states the philosophy involves 'everyone, managers and workers alike'. Unsurprisingly, hugely successful brands such as Toyota lean into Kaizen as a company standard, but it can just as effectively be put into practice at home, within your relationships, or even in the gym.*

The pursuit of continual improvement is something we've long embraced at ThruDark. In its most basic form, this has meant working with the most up-to-date fabrics and employing procedures that minimize waste and/or maximize productivity. We've also worked hard to improve workplace morale, environmental awareness and quality control. Overhauls on the way in which we strategize and debrief have taken place too. As an ideology, Kaizen has worked wonders for us.

There is a caveat, however: when applying Kaizen it's important to understand that this is a slow process rather than a quick fix. It won't deliver overnight success or instantaneous results. But if applied correctly, it will revolutionize your life...

I first stumbled across the idea of Kaizen during the early phases of ThruDark, at a time when I was devouring as much information as I could on start-up culture and business launches. I soaked up different kinds of knowledge via books, podcasts and TED Talks, and when Kaizen was first mentioned, the concept of continual improvement stuck with me for two reasons:

1. I loved Japanese culture, its rich history in martial arts and the way of the Samurai.

2. The idea that a person could live in a perpetual state of growth had already been suggested to me by military service, where every individual was expected to strive tirelessly for personal improvement.

I knew first hand that an attitude like Kaizen required hard work. Willpower and resilience were important too, as were dedication and patience, because success in the military rarely happened overnight. An operator learning the various skills needed to blow through a wall rarely completed what was a large playbook of techniques in several hours. Instead, their mastery happened over time and with practice, often while working in the heat of a battle where there was zero opportunity to flounce off if things weren't working out as hoped. It was their job to stick to the training programme and *improve continually*.

Without knowing it, I'd been working with Kaizen my whole career, and on my first day in the military, I was regarded by my superiors as a know nothing, done nothing. But this was a positive: I was malleable, like a block of clay in the hands of a ceramicist, and so I had potential. In those early days at Commando Training Centre Royal Marines, I was forced to consider who I was and what I was capable of. I came to realize that I was a long way away from being the finished product. There were plenty of miles to cover and I would have to work for all of them, but I had the heart for it – and the patience.

What followed was an intense, thirty-two-week programme where continual improvement was forced upon everybody. We were assessed on our skills and fitness levels. Subtle improvements were noted (they were always subtle improvements that happened over weeks, not minutes or hours), but never celebrated, and our learning took place in increments. At the start of the course, the thought of sprinting over the infamous assault course in Bottom Field, or operating in a smoke-filled mock battlefield seemed unlikely. But having baby-stepped our way to it through training and the introduction of various skill sets, we were able to tackle those challenges effectively when they arrived. By the end, we were equipped with the tools to operate effectively in combat and awarded our coveted Green Berets.

This type of learning was taken up a notch in the military elite, and the types of skills required to succeed had to be performed to the highest level. There was one major difference though: the onus was on the individual to learn those skills themselves, rather than having the relevant information spoon-fed to them. Instructions weren't screamed out across a parade square, they were imparted calmly and it was expected that we absorb them. Likewise, I was sent off on courses where I was required to pick up all sorts of abstract skills that might help me, or my unit, out of a tricky spot in battle. That was because the top tier group I was working in expected us to think outside the box, to work off the cuff when our best-laid plans were falling apart, and to grow into an adaptive and highly functional warrior asset, especially when things weren't going our way.

Training led us forward. One method of creating a cohesive team ethic was to have the lads move in the dark. This was done so that every individual could learn what was expected of them whenever they moved into urban areas, or entered into properties occupied by enemy forces. To prepare us, a body of men would run through their training drills in a pitch-black room, wearing night vision goggles and communicating with subtle hand gestures. It was an eerie thing to be involved in as several operators slipped from room to room in absolute silence.

To make these drills even more realistic, another group would be tasked to act as enemy fighters and it was their job to catch us. However, they weren't equipped with optics equipment and the common reaction during the debriefs that followed was always one of unease: *We knew you were there. We could sense you; sometimes we could even hear you. But we couldn't see anything*. During these sessions I often found myself moving almost in a 'flow state', such was our expertise, and my actions happened instinctively, cued up by the body language of another operator, or in the way a teammate raised their weapon. At times it felt as if we were moving through the space like water, running through gaps and covering the corners.

However, the concept of Kaizen really came into focus during my time as a sniper. As I've mentioned previously, I was a pest for detail, constantly adapting my kit and clothing to suit the environment I was working in. I'd dull down the metal objects on my person to prevent any shine or glinting that might take place in the sun; any rattling objects were locked down tight, and my kit was dyed and dusted so I could stalk through the terrain unseen. The practical results of the Kaizen approach to camouflage and concealment got me out of trouble on more than one occasion, and I remember situations where I would move through whatever ground we were working in at the time to take up an observation position. This was always a risky business. Whenever I moved in that way – whether in training or in conflict – I always felt exposed and I knew if the enemy caught sight of me or my equipment (because it hadn't been disguised very well), I'd have been picked off quite easily.

There were times when I was only 50 metres away from a target, or targets, as they went about their business, completely unaware that I was nearby. Thankfully my kit was sprayed in such a way that it always blended into the environment around me. To anyone mooching around I was pretty much undetectable, though I wasn't invisible and I always knew that the slightest noise or movement at the wrong time would give away my position to a hostile force. It was for that very reason that attention to detail was so important. I had to blend into the environment, my position cloaked by dye and fabric. My knees, elbows and belly protected from the sun-blasted ground by patches of old tent fabric held fast with stitching and superglue.

Those years of continual improvement allowed me to avoid detection throughout my career, leaving me to fight another day.

* * *

When applying Kaizen to our practices at ThruDark, we've followed a fairly standard path. Continual self-improvement has become king, and during the early days, we spent pretty much all our time learning about the finer aspects of design, distribution, fabrics and functionality. Once the company established itself, we turned our HQ into a business hybrid that incorporated a warehouse, creative hub and play area where we could train and spar. I took up the Brazilian close combat martial art jiu-jitsu in that very space. We overhauled the company website to reflect our brand story and identity, and we worked to tweak our management of goods, in and out, so we could reduce time and unnecessary over-processing.

But it was during our product testing phases that the Kaizen philosophy was truly applied and we learned that, when it came to battle-testing the kit, there was really no substitute for personal experience. Rather than just talking up our product, we wanted to push it to the extreme in some of the harshest conditions imaginable. That's why, in 2021, when Nims Purja asked me to join him on an expedition to Ama Dablam – a technically challenging 6,812-metre high peak in Nepal – I decided it was the perfect environment in which to run a series of field tests on our latest summit suit. I also wanted to be bold, to push myself out of my comfort zone by taking on a gnarly climb. The expedition would stretch my physical and psychological limits to the max.

Ama Dablam might not be the tallest mountain in the Himalayas, but it's certainly one of its most challenging. At times I found myself climbing over mixed terrain while using an ice axe and crampons, my body fighting against a sheer drop of 2,000 metres. The mental tussle with fear was very real and at points, I knew that one slip or a misplaced step would have seen me plunging to my death. More than anything though, I had to put a huge amount of faith in my kit: the ice axe, my jumars, ropes, crampons etc. There was no room, or time, to switch off on the mountain. As an expedition, Ama Dablam was an absolute headfuck.

I came through it though, as did the clothing, and when I moved across the mountain, I discovered one or two technical areas that needed improving. In many ways, these were details that, potentially, 99.9 per cent of our customers wouldn't have even noticed, *but I did*, and if ThruDark was to stick resolutely to the Kaizen philosophy, we would have to address them. One issue was the summit suit's mouthpiece, which covered much of my face. It worked well in the icy cold at the top of the mountain, but having topped out and turned around for home, I began sweating heavily while passing through the lower stages of Ama Dablam. This was partly my fault: I wanted to have some great pictures of the suit in action for the website. (In no way would I have worn a summit suit on the lower stages of the climb ordinarily.) But it was a note to take home nevertheless and when I returned, we made design changes to the face veil, so it could be taken off the hood and stored inside the jacket.

More importantly, as a result of the expedition I'd planted a flag for ThruDark by showing that, not only did we *think* our product was next level, we could prove it. This was the brand I lived and breathed. I didn't want us to rest on our laurels until we'd stood apart from our competitors. Adopting Kaizen gave us a fighting chance at hitting that target.

ACTION ON
Becoming Kaizen

I'm not saying you should put your life at risk by climbing a mountain to embrace the concept of Kaizen. I'm not even suggesting you should spend shitloads of cash to test out an idea or philosophy. What I am saying is that your product and practices should be examined under the harshest spotlight – and in realistic conditions – if you're to discover new ways to improve and progress. At this point you're probably wondering '*how?*' So I've put down a few ideas. Maybe something will resonate with you or your situation…

1. **Perform a brutal self-assessment**
   Are you the type of person that tends to arrive late to the office? Do you struggle to see ideas through to the end? Do you flash at the first sign of conflict? Make a note of your flaws and see where improvements can be made – then address them. If you're unable to locate your issues, find someone you know and trust to list your strengths and weaknesses. (Just make sure not to take their criticisms personally.) As a side note, this process can be applied to other aspects in your life:

   - **Relationships**: is there someone you need to reconnect with?
   - **Nutrition**: how can you reduce the unhealthier aspects of your diet?

- **Fitness**: what part of your game needs improvement?
- **Finances**: check your direct debits and cancel the subscriptions you rarely use.
- **Personal development**: is it time to learn a new skill or discipline?

2. **Remember: tiny changes lead to big improvements**
Kaizen doesn't require you to make sweeping changes, only small ones. Example: say you're a writer who finds it hard to locate their creative rhythm in the morning. Commit to getting just 100 words on the page. It doesn't matter if those words are good, bad or ugly, as it's only going to amount to a paragraph or two. The important thing is that you write them down. There's a good chance those 100 words will grow into 150, 200 or 300 with very little effort. Over time those blocked mornings will transform into productive sessions.

3. **Assess your victories and defeats**
We'll discuss the concept of the hot debrief in greater detail later on in the book, but as a starter, it's important to assess the results of your latest project or mission, while everything feels fresh. *How did it go? Where did you do well? What hitches did you encounter?* Find solutions to existing problems by first examining the flaws and screw-ups and then working to correct them. Likewise, any breakthroughs or unexpected successes should be discussed and maximized for future efforts. Make this a regular part of your working process.

4. **Ask questions…**

   … All the time:

   Is this working?

   Can I improve in this area?

   How do I correct this problem?

   Where can we be better, leaner, stronger?

   Becoming Kaizen lies in the answers.

5. **Show patience**

   Kaizen is about continual, but gradual, improvement rather than overnight success. Don't stress if you can't see immediate results, this is not a quick fix app. Instead, find joy in your processes and trust that you'll emerge a more productive asset by staying the course. The key here is consistency.

DEBRIEF

◆ When practising Kaizen, remember to make incremental tweaks rather than sweeping changes. Say you're looking to improve your nutritional intake – have a meat-free Monday rather than trying to go full-blown vegan.

◆ Get uncomfortable. As you progress, put your new skills to the test at a level that will challenge you.

◆ Assess your strengths and weaknesses. Try to build on the positives and work to overcome the negatives.

7

THE UNDERDOG ADVANTAGE

The underdog is a classic trope in many narratives, including sport, business, adventure and even religion. Meanwhile, the David and Goliath story has been taught to kids at school for years. But why?

The truth is that, in its purest form, the underdog tale fills everyone with a sense of hope. It tells us that we can achieve anything on our day. In sport, small teams have beaten established giants, and unknown athletes have taken world champions by surprise at the finishing line. In the hype that follows, there's sometimes a misconception that these events have happened through sheer luck. The reality, as I've learned in my military career, is that the underdog possesses a unique tactical position and if exploited they can turn their greatest weakness into a massive strength.

In war, the fighting force with a 'nothing to lose' mentality is a dangerous proposition, especially if they've been underestimated. And with a little creative thinking they can ultimately become an adversary to be reckoned with. This same spirit applies to business:

when ThruDark began we were a small start-up that relied on the goodwill of our founding investor and some high-profile allies. But with heart, creativity and belief we utilized the underdog mentality with one or two tactical manoeuvres and established a healthy position within the market…

For much of my life I've felt like the underdog. Being bullied at school; my parents' break-up; my mum passing away unexpectedly: as far as I was concerned these weren't the life events usually experienced by champions. (Though they were *exactly* that. Those truths just weren't being told in the stories I used to watch and read as a lad.) The result of these emotional setbacks was the creation of an inner desire to punch upwards and to prove to anyone that was bigger, older or stronger than me that I was an adversary to be feared. I took that attitude on to the football pitch and into the kick-boxing ring; it later fired me up during my time in the military. I had a spark that, when twinned with an intense determination to succeed, helped me to push through moments of pain in tests where most candidates were expected to buckle under pressure.

The Marines showed me that possessing an underdog spirit was an asset. I could harness it as fuel and drive myself on through moments of pain. When the military elite later accepted me into their ranks, the union seemed about right. Selection carried a high failure rate, so it made sense that someone like me would grit their teeth through the discomfort and thrive – *because nobody was stopping me from getting to where I wanted to be.* Once inserted into battle, I then discovered that the top tier of active service was regularly pitched into against-all-odds events and despite our

THE HARD ROAD WILL TAKE YOU HOME

technological might, the units I served in were often heavily outnumbered on missions. Though these operations were always meticulously planned, they often went sideways very quickly, especially if our enemies were able to regroup and strike back in numbers. This forced the lads involved into an underdog position, but I felt OK with that because emotionally it's where I'd spent my whole life. Misfortune had taught me when and how to bite down on my gumshield.

This spirit also helped when starting up ThruDark, and in the early days I had the piss taken out of me for daring to dream differently to some of the other blokes departing from the military. They were heading into personal security gigs and consultancy, and some people couldn't get their heads around my plans to start a clothing brand. As far as the lads were concerned, Louis and I were walking away from a dream life where we got to play with boys' toys, visit the world's most hostile environments and live out a series of Jason Bourne-style adventures. We often heard other operators sniggering whenever we spoke about our ambitions for the company, and one or two people would crack jokes about where we were heading. They still do. Recently we supplied a military team with product specifically designed to function in extreme cold conditions. One operator picked up a jacket and pulled a face.

'Well, it's good clothing, it's decent,' he said, 'but nobody wears this stuff in the mountains—'

His mate cut him off. 'Are you fucking mad? What do you mean, nobody wears it in the mountains? *Nobody like Nims Purja?*'

I laughed. I'd long known that there were people in life who wanted to watch the world burn because they were unhappy with their own lot – they were the type to become bullies and as a kid, I'd grinned at them and punched back. In business I turned the pain into positive action and the gags at my expense became inspirational; they fired me up to work even harder. *And what was the worst that could happen?* Sure, I might lose a lot of money if things went south, in which case the experience would prove humiliating. (And if that happened there was every chance I'd have to go back to my old job and soak up the jokes from my old teammates.) But when I thought about it, these hurdles were nothing compared to some of the scrapes I'd endured in war. I'd successfully executed missions where vital equipment was damaged or destroyed at the worst possible time; when our resources were depleted unexpectedly, or the forces we were coming up against were much stronger than our intelligence had suggested.

In unexpectedly disastrous moments, where the odds of mission success were worsened considerably, we often leant upon a process that was cutely referred to as 'CAKE'. The term was actually a mnemonic, which, when broken down, represented four key actions:

C: Concurrent activity
A: Anticipation
K: Knowledge of systems
E: Expectation / Efficiency

As soon as anything went wrong, the CAKE system sprang into action and it helped us to transform our underdog status into an advantage.

CONCURRENT ACTIVITY: If, say, we were massively outnumbered and outgunned on the ground – and with no real way of escaping – our escape route would be planned by a senior commander and we would be extracted. We would be able to move away from trouble immediately afterwards.

ANTICIPATION: A lot of this work was done in advance, when our orders were first dispatched to us on base. We were told what to do should the group experience heavy casualties, how to move if a target escaped, and how to turn the fact we were a small, but highly effective team to our advantage.

KNOWLEDGE OF SYSTEMS: In times of trouble we always made an assessment of all the resources at our disposal. Weapons systems were evaluated, as were the skill sets among the personnel left scrapping on the ground. We would plan from there.

EXPECTATION / EFFICIENCY: Questions were asked: *Had our situation changed in terms of achieving our objective?* If the answer was 'no' we were to proceed with the job as planned. If the answer was 'yes', we would rethink accordingly. This was when our underdog mentality kicked in. We knew our capabilities as force multipliers. In terms of numbers we represented a small footprint on the ground, but the individual skills within the group and a collective power amplified our influence. At times, we could make a ten- or twenty-strong elite unit feel like a small army.

I had survived plenty of scrapes because the people I served with understood the power of the underdog, Louis too, and we used those experiences to keep our spirits high when things seemed set against us in business. For example, we were able to react to mistakes or delays quickly, such as when a producer was unable to deliver materials on time, without too much fuss or drama. When things became financially hairy, we lifted one another's morale, and used any overheard criticism as propellant, especially when our kit was mocked by the individuals we'd once fought alongside. Weirdly, their tune quickly changed when ThruDark clothing started to gather a serious rep a year or so later. The naysayers started singing our praises then. They wanted to wear the kit. Not that I paid too much attention to the accolades. In much the same way that I'd ignored their snarky comments while we were making our first steps, I ignored the hype whenever we landed major successes. These weren't the people I counted on for validation.

As a kid I'd learned to not value the opinions of bullies.

* * *

Around the time ThruDark began operating, I remember settling down on the sofa with my now wife, Ruby, for the evening as she watched some reality TV show. Half listening, half not, I overheard one contestant as they described them- selves as being 'an influencer'. At the time, I couldn't get my head around it.

'An influencer?' I laughed. '*What the fuck is that?*'

I honestly assumed they'd been taking the piss. But then Ruby asked me why I was laughing. 'These people are making a lot of money,' she said.

When I dug into it, I realized that, yeah, these individuals *were* making a ton of cash by plugging products and experiences, and on very little resources. They'd figured out that all they needed to stick it to the big boys – the TV presenters and giant advertising brands – was an Instagram account, a smartphone and maybe some fancy lighting kit for their home studios. Other than that, the overheads were incredibly small and yet they were gathering more attention on social media than some multi-million-pound companies. People with very little experience, or resources, had figured out how to manipulate the system to their own advantage, and in order to establish ThruDark, Louis and I realized that we would have to think in pretty much the same way – *like underdogs*. We attacked the process with three strategies in mind:

TACTIC No. 1
Reframe Your Status

As a smaller entity, it's easy to feel overawed by the more established competition – or enemy – in the market. But start-ups unsettle established names all the time; they become disruptors, and through effort and tactical thinking, once fledgling entities such as Spotify, Uber and PayPal have been able to change the way people think about them and their industry. However, one thing that unites every emerging business that hits the big time is the fact that they rarely lose heart. Instead they enjoy their moment as a minnow and feed off the benefits of being a smaller team.

So how can you do this? Well, rather than moaning about how you don't have the financial muscle enjoyed by a company the size of, say, Apple or adidas, reframe your relatively small status by maximizing the differences that define you, in much the same way that a non-league team likes drawing a Premier League giant in the FA Cup. In that example, the less wealthy club always turns their perceived poverty into a weapon. The boggy pitch at a semi-professional club is no way near the standards expected by an internationally famous player and it acts as a great leveller. As do the poky dressing rooms and the intimidating terraces. It's little surprise there have been so many giant-killing results over the years.

Remember this: when scrapping as an underdog there will be many moments to enjoy, despite your status, and these moments will propel the business. It might be that you've opened a small grocery store in a town dominated by a large supermarket brand. Rather than being overwhelmed by the size of the competition, work as insurgents and instead connect with the local community – a process that large chain stores can often struggle to do due to their massive turnover of staff. Build personal relationships with your local suppliers and link with the other stores in your street by sharing information, resources and product. Underdogs are most dangerous when they understand their status, so act accordingly. Because going up against the bigger kids in the playground – on their terms, not yours – is the fastest way to a nasty beating.

TACTIC No. 2
Attack Fast; Attack Light

In a conflict, guerrilla-style fighting groups often move quickly and with pared back resources; they improvise to the circumstances around them while learning new tactics and techniques, mainly by watching how their enemies act. But an underdog business can operate in much the same way because its size and status delivers a number of logistical advantages over the more established players in the market. For starters, a company with only four or five employees carries more manoeuvrability than a big-name brand. That means if a brilliant design concept or product idea comes to them overnight, the smaller entity can put their plans into practice very quickly, rather than having to run the suggestion through various layers of bureaucracy and red tape.

But this concept also applies if ever disaster strikes (which it always does) because problems can be resolved quickly and with the minimum amount of fuss. One example of this took place in 2022 when a number of companies were hit by the rising cost of inflation. With an increase in the demand for materials, plus the soaring price of transportation costs, various industries were faced with rocketing overheads and found themselves in a very uncomfortable financial position. This presented two options:

1. The business pushed ahead as normal. The costs were then passed on to the consumer through an increase in product price. (A move that was unlikely to win any popularity contests.)

2. Transport costs were reduced by using shipping, road haulage and train routes, rather than airlines. Yes, this added more time to the production chain but at least the customer wasn't paying any increase.

Having settled on a strategy, the start-up company would have been able to change course almost immediately, while implementing a series of flexible, cost-saving ideas.

At ThruDark, we've worked through one or two moments where products have been delayed for various reasons, sometimes by weeks. Rather than burying our heads in the sand and hoping that the customers won't notice or mind, we've sent personalized letters to each one, explaining the situation while offering refunds. Companies like North Face or Helly Hansen can't work in this way because of the size of their business. They would have to send out thousands of personalized notes, which would prove both costly and time-consuming. The smaller start-up is different though: like a ragtag army landing blows on a military superpower, it can make progress in moments of adversity by thinking quickly on its feet.

TACTIC No. 3
Create a Flexible Fighting Force

The beauty of leading a guerrilla-style business is that it's possible to implement flexibility throughout the team you're working with. Rather than having to manage large numbers of staff that have been shoved into rigid positions – as happens in larger companies – a smaller group can be packed with individuals that are both multi-skilled and willing to work across a range of areas. This is much the same in insurgent forces where the workload is shared across a variety of roles – such as gunman, demolitions expert, informant, spy and so on – and the UK's military elite, which is a more compact and reactionary group where multi-tasking and the learning of new techniques is forever being encouraged.

These strategies are just as applicable to guerrilla-style businesses where resources are tight. For example, you might construct your team so that everyone within it has the talent to work across a wide range of positions. That way, if somebody goes sick (or takes holiday leave at a busy time), or if one area of the business is unexpectedly overwhelmed and requires reinforce-ments, people can move into different positions to provide support. It might be that your social media expert has gone sick on a day of high online activity. In which case, simply ask your most social media-savvy individual from the sales team to take up the reins. If your product manager is suddenly unable to take a meeting with an important client, another team member can step in to handle the conversation, and so on. This flexibility needs to extend to the team leaders too. As I've said before, it's never a bad thing if the boss is seen to be sweeping out the warehouse, especially when the chips are down.

In a final note, it helps to create a culture of initiative by incentivizing the players on your team to learn new skills and pick up the slack when the pressure is high. We'll discuss the concepts of unity and shared values later on in the book, but for now it's worth knowing that the simplest of gestures, little moments of recognition, can help to empower the people working around you. In my office, we have a jokey, ancient-looking scroll that sits in a frame and serves as an Employee of the Week Award. The recipient has to keep it on their desk until another individual does something of note. It might look like a bit of a piss-take from the outside, but it actually means a lot – it's important to us that hard work is rewarded with a bit of recognition. It also serves as a reminder to everyone else that they should always strive to be better.

ACTION ON
Swallow Your Pride

When operating in the theatre of conflict, guerrilla forces often rely upon favours from other like-minded groups and individuals in order to secure money, weapons and various resources. In much the same way, an underdog industry shouldn't be afraid of asking for a little help here and there, whether that be advice or information, or even the sharing of contacts. This process might feel uncomfortable at first, but it's vital to leave your ego at the door. A leg-up from a solid ally can potentially restore the odds in your favour during challenging moments.

As with most guerrilla forces, ThruDark was sometimes low on financial resources during our early days and so we often spent the money coming to us from our investor in a very shrewd way. Nothing was wasted. This attitude forced us to think highly creatively, and in much the same way that an under-resourced fighting group would imagine new ways to attack and defend, so we established smart methods for pushing out our product. Having taken our cue from the aforementioned influencer on reality TV, it was decided we should utilize the free platforms at our disposal, such as Instagram and Facebook, as we rolled out the brand. However, throwing down a few well-shot photographs wasn't enough. We needed to reach a much broader audience instead and that would need us to think smarter.

It was decided that Louis and I should release a (relatively) low-budget, inception film of ourselves as we abseiled down a waterfall in ThruDark kit. On its release, a number of our high profile allies shared the link online, which elevated our name to an even greater level. Promotion of this kind delivered credibility in the marketplace and as the film gained more and more views, and with it, more likes and shares, our credentials were estab-lished: we were former military elite operators-turned-creators, building clothing for the harshest conditions on earth. It helped that our identities were disguised in the images. ThruDark initially carried a mysterious allure; I'd like to think it still does. But by playing with the limited resources at our disposal, and asking for favours, we announced our arrival in an interesting way.

Who and how you ask for help is entirely dependent on your situation, and every business or individual will vary greatly in their requirements and contacts. But there's only one rule to a strategy of this kind: be sure to help out if someone else in a similar position asks for assistance, because that's how the altruistic merry-go-round keeps turning.

DEBRIEF

- Be honest with yourself. If you're not a big player in the market, don't strategize like one. You won't overtake a much stronger opponent on their terms.

- Think like an underdog by moving fast and light, being adaptive to change and building flexible teams.

- Get creative. *What sets you apart from the bigger players in your field?* Find the differences and turn them into an advantage.

8

CONTACT

In military terms, contact is considered to be the exchange of fire between two military forces – or, in other words, the moment on a job when life gets noisy. This generally happens in one of two ways. The first is a strike that takes place at a time of our choosing; the second when an enemy group starts the attack.

Before any sort of pre-planned contact is initiated with a hostile force, the UK military will gather together as much intelligence as possible to determine how and when to engage. This information will include – among other things – the enemy's strengths and weaknesses, their size, the types of weapons systems in their possession and the overall size and positioning of their resources.

When couched in a business setting, however, contact can be used to define a proactive effort, such as a company launch. And as in war, it's beneficial to assess your competitors' strengths and weaknesses (as well as your own), the state of the market and the gaps within it, and the commercial opportunities worth exploiting. However, the procedures used in contact situations can also be applied to a reactive event, such as the response to a moment of chaos or disaster.

Interestingly, one thing links both the planning of covert military strikes and business plans: nobody really hears about them when they go well, but if an operation, or product launch, crashes and burns it can make for some ugly headlines.

In the military, the golden rule when engaging with an enemy is that 'No plan survives contact'. I've been on all sorts of missions where we've ended up attacking a more heavily guarded area than expected and a proactive strike has been suddenly flipped into a reactive event. Those moments, while ugly, are rarely surprising because the British military instils a mindset within every serving asset where the unexpected is expected at all times. One training technique that regularly reinforced this position was the 'false ending', in which a group of operators were told that their work was done for the day, but as their road vehicle drove back to base, and the lads chatted excitedly about a warm bunk and a round of 'hot wets and stickies',* they would come under attack from a mock enemy group. Suddenly they were expected to endure several hours of evasion in the pissing rain. During these moments of psychological discomfort it was important for the individual to adjust, reassess the situation and act accordingly in three steps:

1. **USE DISCIPLINE:** Control the situation with return fire where possible and adjust the plan.

---

* Tea and cakes.

2. **FOCUS:** Train your attention on the things you have at your disposal and figure out how best to use those resources to your advantage.

3. **EXECUTE:** Follow through the next set of tasks to the best of your ability.

Interestingly, this process can be applied to all manner of chaotic events. One time, when I was diving, I got myself into trouble in a powerful current. Sunk in the churn of some dark sea and attached to a dive buddy by a line, I spun and twisted violently underwater. It was night-time; I couldn't see shit so I couldn't exactly call out for help. Mother Nature had me squeezed in her grip: I was pulled this way and that and for a split second I'd felt the eerie sensation of weightlessness before the whirlpooling tide propelled me forward, yanking my body around like a ragdoll.

And then… *Disaster.*

In the spin cycle, my right hand had become pinned across my chest, crushing one of the tubes attached to my rebreather air supply. I used discipline to remain calm. Several years of muscle memory helped and I kept it together pretty well during what was several frantic, potentially overwhelming seconds of disaster. I recalled one or two key techniques from dive training as the world spun around me; phrases, pointers and reminders picked up from military life where I'd been told that I could survive in a situation when the odds were most definitely stacked against me.

Experiences x 1000 = experienced.

How we do anything is how we do everything.

The hard road will take you home.

Then I refocused.

To survive I'd have to act fast by cutting the rope away with my knife, which was attached to my leg. Then I could swim to the surface. But given my right hand was stuck fast, just the process of grabbing it was going to be hard work. I clawed at the hilt.

My first reach was a miss – *no joy*. The effort caused my heart to race even faster and my lungs ached as they strained for air. My cheeks were now puffed out like a hamster.

I had another go – *but it was too much*. I became light-headed. Darkness gathered at the borders of my vision, which meant unconsciousness, and probably death, was closing in.

With one last try I lurched desperately, pulling my knees towards my torso – *and third time lucky!* With my knife released, I hacked at the line and felt myself being pulled away by the currents. Then I kicked with my fins and broke the water's surface, choking and gasping as I sucked in a rush of cold air. A support craft quickly sped into view, and a pair of hands reached down to help.

I heard laughing. 'Hey, you nobber!' someone shouted. 'Why did you come up?'

Then a handheld torch illuminated my face. I was a snotty mess. 'Fucking hell,' said the same voice. 'You look like a ghost.'

There was little doubt in anyone's mind that I'd been in serious trouble, but I'd escaped a potentially fatal situation by running through that simple three-step procedure: *Discipline. Focus. Execution.*

I've since learned that this process works pretty well in all sorts of uncomfortable business circumstances, such as the arrival of a nasty invoice or bill, a dispute with an important contact, or the much-feared 'black swan event',* such as a political upheaval or financial crash. In many ways, these situations can make you feel as if you're under attack, but as in conflict, it helps to:

1. Remain disciplined in an unexpected moment of stress
2. Focus on what you can control and make tweaks where necessary and
3. Deliver on your new plan as best you can.

Really, the emotional processes required to survive are no different to being unexpectedly bumped by a hunter force on a training exercise.

Remember, no matter what's going on in life, the decision on *how* to react rests with you. Losing your head and acting without thinking can be disastrous, and when it comes to executing missions, the elite operator knows to not rush into a hail of rounds and bomb blasts without a plan – death is the best way to screw up a job after all. Instead, when dealing with a stressful reactive situation, it's sometimes advantageous to wait for the smoke to clear around you before establishing a tactical picture of what's happening, rather than sprinting towards failure.

The coronavirus pandemic of 2020 was a classic example of this. As the world closed for business at the beginning of the

---

* The business website Investopedia describes a black swan event as: 'An unpredictable event that is beyond what is normally expected of a situation and has potentially severe consequences. Black swan events are characterized by their extreme rarity, severe impact and the widespread insistence they were obvious in hindsight.' Examples of black swan events would include a stock market crash, war, pandemic or natural disaster.

outbreak, a number of stock traders panic sold their assets as the market began to tank, and at a massive loss. Some companies, fearing the worst, immediately closed down, or laid off their staff too quickly. But had they stayed disciplined and taken a breath to adjust and reassess rather than making knee-jerk decisions, there's every chance some alternative solution might have been found. New plans could have been established; jobs might have been saved; and those panic sellers would have seen the markets rebound later on in the year. (Though I'm aware that for some people, there was no other choice but to close positions and businesses. I'm arguing against those that folded instantly, without considering their options.)

But there were also examples of companies that re-evaluated and pivoted while coming under attack – and to great success. Restaurant owners explored the benefits of turning to takeaway and delivery services. Businesses looked inwards and figured out new ways of improving their online income. Others seized the opportunity to make their systems even more effective. In those cases, a new plan sometimes presented itself fairly quickly. In my industry, for example, companies were able to focus on their online trade only, and at ThruDark that meant our current business practices could remain in place. Really, all we had to do was figure out:

1. How to work safely together
2. Who would work from home and who would physically come into the building, and
3. What adjustments our distributors and manufacturers were making and whether we should react accordingly.

As a clearer picture of the pandemic took shape, we were able to adapt slowly, but steadily.

* * *

As I stated earlier, the best way to make a proactive strike in war is to first assess the enemy by using the intelligence at your fingertips. This was collected in all sorts of ways and by working through the resources at our disposal we were able to assess the strengths and weaknesses of our enemy before making a call on how best to deal with them.

But there are one or two basic guidelines for what *not* to do when preparing to strike. One of them regards the obvious failure of not preparing properly – either by neglecting to gather together an appropriate amount of intelligence, or by overlooking a vital piece of information. The other regards timing. It is *everything* in both business and in war. And just as a mistimed attack can leave a military force kicking through a dry hole (our term for an abandoned enemy base, or hideaway), so a poorly thought out H-hour* or poorly informed business decision can leave a company floundering. For example, innovative products have sometimes launched ahead of their time and died on the vine; others have arrived too late and then failed to make an impact as the world moved on. Then there are those products that simply got released in a bit of a muddle due to the creators having been caught up in

---

* For anyone reading this who isn't overly familiar with military phrases, H-hour is a term used to reference a time of strike. For example, '*H-hour for dropping on to target is 0200*.' At that moment, everything is supposed to come together – on the ground, in the air, and from the other assets in play.

a logistical mess. I know this all too well because ThruDark once released an Arctic-proof parka in the height of summer.

In our defence, we were still fairly green. Throughout 2017, having studied the market and gathered together a hefty amount of intelligence from our business contacts, we planned for a company launch around Christmas time. At that point we wanted to unveil our website and release three styles of coat, one of which was the aforementioned parka, and everything was planned out on the company whiteboard. Product designs were in place and a schedule had been agreed with fabric manufacturers, distributors and website designers. A doable, six-month schedule was established, with an added fortnight of 'fudge time' in case one or two things went awry. As far as I was concerned, we'd laid out a rock-solid battle plan. Sadly it hadn't been anywhere near solid enough.

Everything that could go wrong went wrong. We were late for production. We were late to release our website. We were late to release our products, which were going to be unveiled at a special event at the flagship London branch of Bremont – the high-end, military-influenced watchmaker – where a number of brand ambassadors were showing up. Before long, a Christmas 2017 launch had been pushed back until May 2018. We were partly at fault for this situation: it was our first product drop and we'd been overly fiddly with the designs. Over a period of months we'd commissioned eight prototypes, and the first seven failed to meet our high demands. Zips needed moving. Pockets were shifted around. At one point the factory must have wondered whether we'd lost the plot. The fudge time we'd added to deal with any delays ebbed away. One or two unexpected hold-ups with our designers and manufacturers later stretched into weeks and then months. It quickly became a horror show.

There had been plenty of opportunities to move the company's Bremont unveiling back even further, but when the option was discussed we'd pushed it to one side, knowing there was never really the perfect moment to launch a company. As we'd already discovered, no plan survives enemy contact and something nearly always goes wrong. I also knew too many people that had previously pumped the brakes on an idea or decision because they'd been waiting for the optimum window of opportunity, but that moment had never arrived and their ideas were then shelved. All the same, the schedule still felt slightly manic, and on the morning of the launch, our website was unfinished. *And the H-hour was rapidly approaching.*

For the entire car journey to London and Bremont, both Louis and I sat hunched over our laptops. I was on the phone, checking the finer details of the website with our developer. Louis was receiving an update on delivery schedules from our manufacturers. It felt like a complete balls-up. And then I remembered we were releasing a winter coat in summertime.

I looked over at Louis. 'At least we'll be stocked up for Christmas,' I said, trying to lighten the mood.

By the time we'd arrived at our hotel to change, a date from our manufacturers had been set in stone. Only our website remained unfinished, but it was just the final details that were being finessed. An hour later, as we walked into the Bremont store and met with our investor, brand ambassadors and supporters, I finally received the text that told me ThruDark was off the hook. Our website was ready.

'That's it,' I said, nudging Louis. 'We've cracked it. We're now live.'

I later realized that the key to succeeding in moments of contact, such as this one, had been our ability to readjust calmly. Louis and I hadn't flapped or rushed into a mistake. We'd simply maintained focus and adapted to any new intelligence by altering our course appropriately. We were then able to complete the job. Emotionally, this launch of ThruDark reminded me of a last-minute mission gone wrong, which they did from time to time, and terrifyingly so. But the operating systems in place to survive them were no different when stripped down to their basic parts.

I've been involved in all sorts of incidents in my military life where plans have been ripped to shreds by an enemy attack and I've had to think on my feet. There were times when I thought I was packing up for the day only for a call to come in saying that we had to conduct another mission, even though we had been scrapping all day long. There were other occasions when I found myself in the wrong position for a helicopter pick up and had to run around in a muddy field while weighed down with equipment in order to find a suitable landing zone. The effort could be pretty draining – and that was before the enemy had opened fire, which they inevitably did. Readjusting and pushing forward in highly volatile situations was always manageable because we'd been taught how to cope emotionally.

You can also prepare for moments of contact in your daily practices, in ways that are both proactive and reactive. All you need to do is establish some stress-tested procedures that will help you to deal with any moments of contact. Examples of these might include:

- Up-armour your mindset. The only way to truly understand how your business is going to cope in a moment of contact is to live through one. However, the only way to live through one is to approach it with an open mind. On the eve of every high-risk plan, or moment of chaos, tell yourself: 'This is going to be a new experience. Things might go pear-shaped, but I'll tough my way through it and learn.' Seriously, the best way to manage this process is by simply thinking and doing. Be open to change. Surround yourself with allies from the field you're in so you can lean on them for advice. A great way to up-armour is through the doing – *so do*.

- Battle-plan an attack: What's the worst that can happen? *Well, why not find out?* In advance of a large business decision, list the danger scenarios within your control. Then figure out if you're in a position to cope should they actually happen.

   This process is used all the time at ThruDark. We refer to it as a 'pre-mortem', and when preparing to launch a new product line we'll ask serious questions of the business to assess our defence against any potential disasters:

   ○ *What happens if we sell out of the new line?*

   ○ *What happens if the supplier can't restock in time?*

   ○ *What happens if we over-order?*

   There's nothing to stop you from running through a similar stress test. However, if you're struggling to find

some potentially worrying scenarios consider the
following examples as jumping off points. (If they don't
fit your situation exactly, tweak accordingly.)

1. At the lower end of the scale, you might have a solid
    connection with your supplier, but what happens if they
    decide to close down their business? *Do you have a backup?*
    Could you strike a deal with another at short notice?

2. At the more troublesome end, what would happen if a
    regular client deal fell through? Or a valuable repeat
    customer decided to look elsewhere? *Do you have enough*
    funds in the bank to keep the business rolling? Do you have a
    list of potential customers to approach? These might sound
    like overly simplistic questions for unpleasant scenarios,
    but game planning your reactions to these events can
    really help to train your emotions whenever contact takes
    place for real.

•   Learn the value of a false deadline. Though the Bremont
    launch was delayed, most of the problems that had
    challenged us weren't really of our making – beyond our
    design changes, we'd also been let down by people who
    were unable to meet our deadlines. This was a frustrating
    process for me. I have high standards when it comes to
    doing whatever I've promised. At the time I also
    understood that lashing out wasn't going to change the
    situation, so instead I reframed my thinking as to how
    other people viewed deadlines and agreements. But while
    there was no point getting angry with someone who didn't

share the same passion for the brand as me, I wasn't going to take a passive approach either. Instead we started setting false deadlines with our contractors, sometimes asking for product to be delivered six weeks ahead of our actual deadline. (Not that we told them.) Remember: H-hours are movable; set them to your advantage.

• Sidebar: There will always be occasions when you'll find yourself working to someone else's deadlines. The good news is that you can create an H-hour for yourself within the established time frame. Say a research document needs to be delivered by a certain date; there's nothing to stop you from setting an H-hour one or two days in advance so that you can have some time to sit with the material, and then finesse and improve where necessary. Just because you're working to the schedule of someone else, it doesn't mean you can't establish a certain amount of control.

ACTION ON
Trust Your Gut

While there are optimal moments to strike, it's often very hard to time a decision perfectly. When deciding exactly when to launch a new product, our decisions have been based on careful analysis (such as our finances, deadlines and other commitments) and the advice of our investor. This intelligence is then used to plan. However, when it comes to the process of choosing an H-hour we've often twinned this information with good old-fashioned gut instinct – the type that has kept me alive during some seriously sketchy moments on the battlefield. And there have been more times than I'd care to remember when I've held back from kicking in a door, or opening fire, because the hairs on the back of my neck have prickled, or an inner voice has whispered: 'Mate, something's not right here...' On one occasion, my decision to hold fire even stopped me from killing an unarmed hostile.

We'd surrounded a home that we suspected was being used by a group of enemy fighters. Having ordered everybody to leave, the gunmen emerged, their hands in the air, and after a moment's pause, I stepped into the house with my weapon raised so I could sweep the place for assets. As I scanned the first room, I noticed a man crouched down in the firing position, and under the circumstances I would have had every right to shoot: we'd ordered everyone to leave the premises peacefully, but this individual had remained behind, and was waiting in a seemingly threatening position. *But something wasn't right.* To the untrained eye it might have looked as if he was about to open fire, but his body shape caused me to stop. In a split second I realized that he was cowering, not preparing to attack. Years of training had taught me to instantly read a person's hands rather than their face, so it was possible to determine their intent. Having not seen a weapon, I instructed the guy to leave, breathing a sigh of relief that I hadn't pulled the trigger.

The poor bloke was clearly terrified and as I stepped out of the building, my team leader walked over. 'Good call, Staz,' he said.

Then he delivered possibly the best piece of advice I'd heard during wartime: 'Don't ever feel like you have to go charging round buildings because of what we are, or you think you've got something to prove. Just trust your gut. Sometimes things won't feel right: that's when you've got to listen to it.'

Those words have kept me sharp in moments of contact ever since. I realized that we'd been trained to the highest level and I'd gained a high degree of battle experience. That meant my subconscious was attuned to making big decisions in moments of high stress. The same can be said of my position now. When things have gone haywire at ThruDark, I've listened to my instincts because my operating system has been sharpened by crazy business launches, black swan events and unreliable suppliers. You can put yourself in a similar position too. Simply *plan and do* to a high standard, as detailed in this chapter. Because with preparation and experience at your back you'll be able to rely upon gut feelings in much the same way – especially when the enemy kicks off unexpectedly.

DEBRIEF

- In moments of chaos remember to:
  - remain disciplined
  - refocus
  - execute your new plan.

- Learn the power of the false deadline. By giving yourself the appropriate amount of 'fudge time' you'll be able to handle any unexpected problems without the added pressure of a ticking clock.

- Up-armour your mindset: the best way to learn is to *do*, so throw yourself into any uncomfortable situations with an open mind.

9

THE CONTROLLABLES

A well-known military saying states that we should only ever worry about controlling the controllables. Or to put it another way: in times of trouble we should strap down as much as we can and only deal with the doomsday scenarios if they actually happen. (Which a lot of the time they probably won't.)

This phrase has since crossed over into business and leadership manuals and while it makes perfect sense when said out loud, actually implementing its core principles can take a bit of work, largely because as humans we've been designed to overthink. We catastrophize and seek out the absolute worst-case scenarios. When they emerge in our thoughts, we dwell on them for way too long until they've festered to such an extent that we lose sight of what actually needs to be done.

In the military, I was trained to concentrate on the overall objectives in hand and not to become distracted by any unexpected factors that might – or might not – cross my path. By implementing

*one or two techniques, which I'll detail here, you'll be able to maintain
a similarly high level of discipline in stressful situations…*

* * *

The problem most people have when it comes to figuring out
how to control the controllables is the understanding of exactly
what's in their control in the first place. If that's the case, they're
usually oblivious to any potential moments of vulnerability
looming on the horizon, and therefore unable to act when an
uncontrollable event does kick off. Having said that, I've found
there's actually a simple way to bring stability to your life and
that's by establishing a plan for yourself in the short, medium
and long term. This might sound like a near-impossible suggestion at first, especially in those moments when your working
practices feel unfamiliar or even out of control. *How are you
supposed to make a schedule for a year or two down the line when
you can't even see past next week?* However, if you can push past
your doubts and plan effectively, you'll soon become the master
of your own destiny. Let me show you how.

The first thing to do when figuring out a plan in the short,
medium and long term is to look beyond your immediate
commitments for a brief moment and focus on the medium-
to long-term goals. So, say you're opening a tattoo studio in a
newly purchased high street location. The first thing to do is
scribble down some rough targets and deadlines so that you
can work towards a tangible end result. That will allow you to
establish a finishing line. From there you'll be able to bolt down
as many moving parts as possible by implementing a military

process known as a Course of Action (COA). This is done in three phases:

1. Identify the opening target – in this case, the opening day of your tattoo studio and the arrival of the first customer.
2. Working backwards, research the processes required to set up a store and to manage the overheads. Create a brand identity; look into how the store could be promoted and explore different methods for attracting new clients.
3. Assess your strengths and weaknesses. Possible strengths: it might be that you have a clear brand vision in place and an experienced tattooist. You might also have a healthy level of investor support. Weaknesses: in managerial terms you're inexperienced and driving semi-blind, so issues such as the launch and the general day-to-day running of the business might cause some teething problems at first.

Once this is done, kick around a series of potentially controllable problems to see if they can be bootstrapped down in advance:

PROBLEM: This is your first tattoo studio. How will you attract new customers?

SOLUTION: *I have a healthy budget. Let's go with a 25 per cent discount for any customers that come in during the first six weeks.*

PROBLEM: What overheads does the business have?

SOLUTION: *List the costs of premises, staff, utilities,*

insurance and so on. Is the company over-extended in any way? If so, is it possible to score a better deal on the monthly bills? And how much does the business have to make to break even every month?

PROBLEM: How will we deal with reduced trade during the week?

SOLUTION: *Offer discounts or incentives, such as complimentary beers, coffees and products for any customers using the service on typically slow days.*

After that, it should be possible for the business to project a rough budget for the coming one or two years by estimating income and costs. Of course, the final figure won't be exact, but it should give the owners an idea of how much they can spend on marketing, promotion and other such things. By taking control of the controllables, any unexpected events that might arise can be handled more effectively.

Louis and I have applied this process to every aspect of business. We understand that there will likely be an uncontrollable event that throws us off course from time to time, so to minimize their impact we've regularly worked from the three lists: one featuring the short term (hours, days), another the medium term (weeks, months) and a final list that focuses on the long term (years one, two and three). Underneath each heading we've scribbled down what we want to achieve, marking the areas that we can actively control – such as the launch of several new products for the following season – before working out how to execute the stages required to get us there. Worrying about issues outside our influence, such as recessions, natural disasters or geopolitics isn't worth the mental calories.

Interestingly, the short-, medium- and long-term strategies can be applied to every aspect of a person's life. I now use it regularly to structure the business, and myself, to such an extent that I'm able to maximize my impact upon the day. I'm organized. I have a clear path from start to finish, and should any unexpected events cross my path, I'm able to readjust quite clearly by moving things around in the short term.

SHORT TERM
THE DAY TO DAY

I set the day out in three-hour windows, listing tasks for myself in each one and then ticking them off as they're nailed. By 8:30 I'm into work and sorting the most pressing issues. For example, I'll analyse the latest sales figures, or edit and approve any social media posts we might have coming down the track. *I like to get the most important shit done first.* The remainder of my work-related windows will be broken down into meetings, photo shoots, Zoom calls, picking and packing orders and training. By the evening, the final window is spent winding down. I'll play with the kids, have dinner with my wife Ruby and relax in front of the telly.

MEDIUM TERM
THE WEEKS AND MONTHS AHEAD

It's in this stage where the deadlines and schedules for the company are pulled together: our achievable targets are listed along with the actions required to achieve them. We'll organize product launches, design meetings and promotional campaigns; names will be assigned to tasks. As we progress, everyone will feed back on the work and over the past few years this has proved to be an ideal way in which to strategize and problem-solve.

LONG TERM
FUTURE GOALS

During this stage we'll figure out what we want to achieve in the coming year and establish a timeline for each target, writing down the monthly tasks that need to be executed in order to land our goals. Deadlines are established and duties assigned. Our list at ThruDark includes:

- Brand identity
- New product launches
- Customer loyalty initiatives
- Trips abroad for promotional photo shoots

At the same time we'll apply a SWOT analysis (strengths and weaknesses; opportunities and threats) to each target. For example, we'll align our ambitions with the company budget to ensure we don't fall into any financial holes. It's all very well saying that you'd like to launch several coats at once and organize a lavish advertising shoot in the Andes, but the accounts might tell a whole other story.

I've found the best way to build these lists is to work backwards from the end goal. *So, where do you want to be a year down the line? The owner of your own business? Promoted to a more senior* position? Widely recognized for your creative efforts? Write your destination down and then work in reverse, figuring out the necessary steps for achieving your overarching aims. I've also found that in a team environment, having a timeline of this kind means that everyone involved is accountable for any failures they might make. As a result they'll become more motivated to hit their targets. These lists also psychologically reward the individual for their successes: tasks can be ticked off and projects can visibly move forward in phases.

If all this sounds mind-achingly obvious, well, *that's because it is* – but you'd be surprised at how many people don't plan out their life in this way. Instead they drift through the days, weeks and months without focus. When disaster strikes they struggle to cope. If an unexpected success falls into their lap they're unable to maximize it in a way that allows them to grow. I've found that the simple act of scribbling down our short-, medium- and long-term strategies on to a whiteboard can turn a thought or ambition into a more tangible target, with structure and a time frame. *It puts me in control.*

At ThruDark, when we plan out our marketing strategies, they'll often feel overly ambitious at first, but through the physical act of list writing – and then immediately strategizing the controllables in the short, medium and long term – those grand plans quickly feel like an accepted reality. Case study: In the winter of 2022, we organized a trip to Morzine, France in order to shoot a new range of mountain wear with some of our ambassadors. We'd done these trips before and they were often incredibly overcomplicated with lots of moving parts. There were nearly always several factors beyond our influence, such as weather conditions and the hectic schedules of everyone involved. However, the job was put in motion by first breaking the mission down into those three timescales and then displaying them in the office so that everyone could see the working phases involved and their responsibilities within them. Moving backwards, these tasks included:

LONG TERM: Let's improve the visibility of the brand and promote our new winter range with a cool photo shoot.

MEDIUM TERM: Photographer and videographer: Who are we going to hire and how do we get them to location? What equipment is needed and how will that kit be transported to site? Which ambassadors are we going to invite? And so on...

SHORT TERM: Where are we going? How do we get there? Where are we staying? How much will it cost?

With this timeline in place, we were able to follow a clearly defined set of tasks until the job was executed and the shoot posted to our website and social media platforms. The military elite had taught us to plan meticulously. By doing so, we were able to comfortably deal with the issues within our control and create some wriggle room for those that weren't. To leave a plan dangling in the wind would need us to rely on hope from time to time. As I've stated previously, that's a course of action I'm not inclined to take.

ACTION ON
Pre-Adjust to the Uncontrollables

There were plenty of things I *could* control when starting Selection. I was able to manage my fitness and preparation, and my kit and equipment; I used my time in the build-up wisely by taking a recce on the hills in Wales and becoming comfortable with map-reading skills and moving across the terrain with some serious weight on my back. What I couldn't control was the weather, and the Hills Phase took place in two seasons:

1. The winter when it was freezing cold and the rain and snow pelted down for days on end, and
2. The summer, when it could be incredibly hot and the terrain offered zero shelter from the sun.

My course took place in the summer. I readied myself for the heat and the sweat by prepping my mind.

How? Well, I worked doubly hard in those months leading into the first day of Selection until I felt mentally and physically ready, and my administration was next level. I put systems in place for eating and drinking while moving around and I trained in the heat so I'd understand how my body and mind were going to respond in those conditions. I then practised packing my Bergen in such a way that I'd have easy access to water, spare maps and a spare compass, plus a medical kit, sewing kit, even extra bootlaces. Some of this stuff I used; some of it I didn't, but being well prepared empowered me.

Of course there were one or two uncontrollable elements that might take place. I could get injured or sick, or the heavens might open in an unexpected storm, but my intense prep told me that in the event of nasty weather I'd stay strong against the elements. I could treat myself if I picked up blisters or sunburn at any point and I would be able to stay rehydrated throughout. Every morning, when waking up, I thought: 'It's going to be scorching hot today. I'm going to be super-tired, dehydrated and hungry.' If the weather panned out that way, then I'd already emotionally set myself up to cope. If the weather turned wet and mild, it felt like a bonus. That lifted my mood even higher.

Often, when we're trying to look into the future (where we tend to imagine the worst-case scenarios), 99 per cent of our imagined outcomes never happen. However, if we've taught ourselves how to climb the metaphorical mountain, we're more likely to survive if the avalanche does take place. By making sure the hatches are battened down tight on what you can control, the uncontrollable feels so much easier to negotiate. So prepare effectively and breathe easy.

DEBRIEF

- Humans like to consider the doomsday scenario. Rather than stressing about any negative events that *might* happen, focus on the things that *definitely will* and make sure they've been squared away. Preparation = confidence.

- When planning for a major task or event, set out what needs to be done in the short, medium and long term, and establish a series of tasks for each. Working backwards from the long term, tick off your activities until the final goal is smashed.

- Make your plans more coherent, and visible, by writing them down, preferably somewhere that's in view at all times. This process alone can be a great motivator.

10

THE ARMOUR OF DAILY HABITS

Habitual behaviour is everything in war and the importance of establishing a positive routine was reinforced on a daily basis while I was serving. It was easy to see why. Not checking my kit before a mission could lead to an oversight, such as a malfunctioning weapon. Not training properly might diminish my fitness levels and combat readiness, while not up-skilling wherever possible would result in me becoming a weak link within the squadron.

Habitual behaviour is also important in positions of business and leadership, because by operating within a positive routine an individual gives themselves the room to thrive, inspire and grow. It's for this reason that many successful entrepreneurs and visionaries extol the virtues of rising early or smashing through their emails first thing in the morning. They also talk about their routines in networking, journaling and meditation. These actions breed positive traits that work as effective tools.

Of course, bad habits are just as contagious as good ones. The trick is to weed out any negative processes before switching them up with a productive alternative. (Idea: try swapping your afternoon snack break for a round of ten squats or push-ups, then eat an apple.) With your vices removed, it's possible to establish a healthy routine that will set you up for progression, from the moment the alarm goes off in the morning to the final social media check of the night…

A culture of routine and accountability was thrust upon me throughout Royal Marines basic training, to the point where it sometimes felt overwhelming. I quickly learned the reason for this intensity. Positive habits, when performed ritually, prepared a commando for long-term success. Meanwhile, the imparted rituals, executed to the highest standard, helped an individual to function when war was at its roughest. Once I'd arrived at Lympstone, I was thrust into a world where my personal administration had to be next level. I picked up my kit and my head was shaved. I was taught how to make my bed and prepare my uniform. The group was even shown the finer details of personal grooming and we were taught how to wash our cocks properly. (Because being incapacitated with crotch-rot in a gunfight wasn't going to help anyone.) Over and over we were told the same thing: slacking and shoddy behaviour was not acceptable.

These habits were instilled through two methods. The first was storytelling and we were taught about the *Compound Interest of Fucking Up*, whereby in an obviously made-up tale, a 'Shit Marine' fails to perform the most basic of personal admin duties. His life then spirals out of control in small increments until he reaches the worst possible ending. *Death*. I can even remember the chief instructor detailing a ludicrous scenario in which the poorly organized commando had failed to clean out his standard issue mug properly.

'It's dirty, but he doesn't care. When he next drinks water out of it, he goes down with a stomach bug and gets the shits. Next thing, he's given the stomach bug to somebody else. When *he* gets it, the whole fucking section goes down. And so we're down a section in a fucking war. Then the company goes down with the stomach bug – *the Shit Marine's stomach bug* – until eventually the entire fighting force has been overwhelmed with illness and we're killed by the enemy... *All because one bellend couldn't clean his fucking mug properly.*'

The example was ridiculous. A lot of the lads found it funny, but it drove home a serious point. Positive habits mattered. *They stopped an individual from screwing up.* But they also laid the foundations for survival. As the Australian author and actor F.M. Alexander* once stated: 'People do not decide their futures. They decide their habits and their habits decide their futures.'

The other way in which lessons were imparted happened in a more painful, and/or humiliating manner, depending on whichever instructor was screaming orders at you in the moment. Mainly we were told what to do, and how and when to do it. Anyone unable to follow a specific set of instructions was physically thrashed, or, much worse, made to watch as their teammates were forced through an extra gruelling physical drill because of their misdemeanour. This was an incredible motivator. I didn't want to

---

* Beginning in the 1890s, Alexander put together the Alexander Technique, which detailed how the habit of poor posture could lead to serious health problems. He had advanced this technique in a successful attempt to reclaim his voice and perform Shakespeare plays.

incur my teammates' wrath by screwing up in some way; I didn't particularly enjoy running around in the pissing rain for an extra hour as a result of some dickhead forgetting to pack their Bergen correctly either. That meant I had to look out for the people around me, while maintaining my personal standards. If somebody was seen to be struggling or slacking off, they were pulled up by the others, and nobody was allowed to cut any corners. Before long, the basic skills were being executed by the group, and to a very high level.

This attitude was dialled up to eleven by the time I'd joined with the elite forces. Having been badged and introduced to my new teammates, I was given a series of checklists. These needed to be executed on a daily, weekly and sometimes monthly basis, and whenever we were at base, or if stationed on domestic duties, the team was forever checking, double-checking and then triple-checking their kit and equipment. Lads tinkered with their stuff, moving equipment pouches here and there. Weapons systems were tested, and bags were packed and repacked. Everything was over-egged – we often joked about having to attend briefings about forthcoming briefings – but that's because the consequences for failure were so bloody high. We needed the technological and procedural odds to be stacked in our favour at all times because they weren't when it came to our physical numbers, and nobody wanted to be the bloke who forgot a vital piece of kit before a mission.

Unlike the regular military, there was nobody to scream insults at me if I slipped up at any point, and psychologically that created a constant pressure to do well. We were a self-policing entity and the onus was on me to stick to my responsibilities; I didn't want to look useless in front of the other lads, operators that I respected and admired. And so I became even more of a kit pest. I kept myself sharp. I looked after my body too, by feeding and watering myself as best I could, while ensuring that I was in top physical condition at all times. For the most part, the hard-core nature of the job maintained my fitness, but in those rare moments of downtime between missions, we'd often visit the base gym for an extra serving of pain.

The mood during these sessions could be intense, but fun, and a great way to tune out the war raging around us. The squadron sometimes worked out in groups, which created a series of funny rivalries among the lads, while building a bond between those that trained together. Whenever an opportunity arose to hit the weights, everyone was expected to be on call, just in case we were unexpectedly ordered into action at the last minute. I can remember one occasion when we'd been told we would be sitting out for two days because one of our helicopters was being repaired. When a mate suggested we go into the gym, I hit it hard. *Big mistake*. It was a leg day, *the worst kind of day*, and I was lifting heavy as we ran through a jamboree of squats and lunges. By the end of the session I'd been blown out, but in a good way, and then, as we drove back to our rooms the call came in. We were being called back urgently.

'Oh shit,' I thought. 'What's all this about?'

The whole group gathered together. According to our senior commander, a top target had popped up in the area and there was only a short window of time to grab them.

'Lads, get your kit together. We're going out now.'

As I sat up, my legs groaned and every muscle seemed fit to

explode. *Had my calves and thighs been injected with concrete?* If I was training at home I'd have enjoyed the sensation – pain often served as a reminder that I'd put in a solid shift. On this occasion, however, I knew what lay ahead. I would be expected to run around while carrying heavy kit and my weapons system before getting involved in a fast-moving operation.

'Fucking hell, my legs are in bits,' I laughed, as we waddled to the equipment cage.

The job involved moving on to target. The fighting was intense and at times I had to run around at top speed. But the adrenaline took the edge off my discomfort and pushed me through. When I finally fell into my bunk that night I was fucked. *But what else was I supposed to do?* Maintaining my strength and fitness was a vital part of my daily routine, and no less important than checking my weapon or washing my balls. I also understood that neglecting my personal responsibilities could trigger a negative chain reaction in personal standards. Or, as my old instructor would have called it, the *Compound Interest of Fucking Up.*

* * *

What does a healthy stack of habits bring to our day to day? In a military sense the intention was to give every commando an edge over the enemy; by maintaining high standards, our hope was that we would be a fitter, more capable and better-prepped force than the other lot. This idea was also true outside the UK Armed Forces. I've since taken an armoury of positive actions into my civilian life and it's paid dividends. With a solid routine I'm able to hit my targets at work and home; I can also avoid sliding into bad habits and laziness. It helps that I'm able to tick off a series of daily commitments (such as conducting a morning briefing in the office, or working out), which creates a rewarding sense of achievement. Finally, I've also learned that a routine, or a chain of positive habits, can be a life raft to grab on to whenever things get messy. If I'm able to get up at the same time and then hit a series of targets throughout the day, it can bring some semblance of order to a shit storm.

These are all great reasons for adding an armour-plated routine to your schedule. The big question is this: *exactly what should I do and why?* I've found that it only takes a short period of planning to establish a routine that fits your goals. So, once you've figured out your long-term targets and planned backwards (as discussed in the previous chapter) you'll find it's possible to build a list of tiny habits that should propel you towards them. In my case, the long-term targets included:

1. Spending quality time with my wife and kids every day; keeping my head straight by resting and recovering in the right way.

2. Maximizing ThruDark's potential; flexing my creative muscles and expanding the business with a brotherhood of teammates.

3. Experiencing physical endeavour through adversity by pushing my body to its limits in training and jiu-jitsu; clearing my head from stress with mates in the ThruDark HQ training area.

Having established my goals, I've since structured my daily habits accordingly:

WAKE-UP CALL: I get up at 7am most mornings. (Full disclosure: I might hit the snooze button occasionally, but that's very rare.) As I've detailed elsewhere, I'll then run through a series of tasks to set my momentum for the day (spending time with my wife and kids at breakfast, walking the dog while listening to a podcast), though the most important habit I have is to make the bed. No matter what's going on in the house, I'll always square away the duvet and plump the pillows, just as I'd been trained in the military. OK, it's a clichéd ritual among business leaders, but this one gesture at the start of the day works as a powerful psychological cue. It reminds me to stay disciplined. However, yours could be plucked from a huge list: stretching, meditation, connecting with a member of the family, working out, or meal-prepping for the day.

Each and every element of what appears to be a basic routine is actually a building block for long-term success. As the author James Clear wrote in his book *Atomic Habits*: 'Changes that seem small and unimportant at first will compound into remarkable results if you're willing to stick with them for years. We all deal with setbacks but in the long run, the quality of our lives often depends on the quality of our habits.

With the same habits, you'll end up with the same results. But with better habits, anything is possible.'

MISSION PLANNING: Once the team has arrived at ThruDark everyone gathers in the Fish Tank for a meeting – a glass-fronted office that overlooks the warehouse space. This is held every morning to make sure that everyone is in good shape and prepared for the day ahead. We'll discuss the most pressing actionable procedures so that we can hit our targets by the end of the day, week and month. We're a direct-to-consumer business so the discussion will always cover product, goods in and out, delivery and finances. Meanwhile, the team is rapidly growing and the individuals within it have their own issues and responsibilities to manage. For example, the product master deals with product. The creatives deal with design, social media and the company website. The photography department does exactly what it says on the tin. These subject matter experts, plus our pay-per-click specialists and financial boffins means there's a lot of stuff working in tandem. A morning briefing is the habit that holds us all together.

TRAINING: When it came to designing ThruDark's company headquarters, it was of high importance to Louis and me that a training space was set up on the property, comprising weight racks, sleds, battle ropes and so on. Positioned in a corner of the warehouse, I'll use this facility at least once a day throughout the week, focusing on jiu-jitsu on Mondays, Wednesdays and Fridays. The other days are mixed up with strength work, high intensity interval training (HIIT) and cardio. I encourage everyone in the company to train, either as a group or individually, and the knock-on effect has been contagious. Most of the group now utilizes the space. As a result we've grown stronger together.

Really the only person that's going to know if you're sticking to a positive routine is an army of one. *And that's you*. So, if putting your plans into action is a stumbling block, or if you're the type of person that lets good intentions slide, I suggest following the path set by recovering junkies, alcoholics and gambling addicts. Rope in an accountability partner for support – a friend, loved one or teammate. Alert them to your plans at an early stage by stating your intentions and overall goals. It might be that you're about to work through a stressful career change, or you're pushing for a promotion, in which case a series of pro-ductive habits will help you through. Maybe your business is haemorrhaging cash and you need to keep a tab on the finances. You'll need to factor in some time to assess the accounts on a regular basis while establishing some belt-tightening measures to keep everything in order.

The accountability partner's role in all of this is to hold you to your aims, so show them your list of necessary healthy habits. They're also supposed to call you out if you slacken off. If you're thinking about skipping an after-work function, it's their job to remind you of the importance of optics and how it might help your promotion chances if you show your face – at least for a little while. If you're considering splashing out on a fancy team meal at Christmas, it's their duty to mention your rising credit card debt. You might think of your accountability partner as a massive buzzkill at first, but if you follow their advice they'll soon get you to where you need to be.

This relationship is particularly powerful when both people are working for a shared cause. Louis and I will often keep each other in check over certain commitments because we both want the business to succeed. Elsewhere, there have been many times when I've wanted to sack jiu-jitsu off for the day having been too tired, or too busy for the scrap. Rather than bailing, I've taken some time to consider the person I usually train with. 'Rolling' around solo on the mat isn't much fun and so I'll imagine my training partner's frustration and disappointment. That has worked as a powerful motivator. Nobody wants to let down a mate or colleague, especially if they're someone you value and respect, so fall into the unbreakable habit of showing up for the people around you.

ACTION ON
Kick the Habit of Procrastination

The irony about struggling to start the process of routine building is that procrastination in itself is a habit. Really, it's not unlike hitting the snooze button five times over in the morning, or skipping the gym and heading to the pub after you've had a bad day at work. According to a talk delivered by the author and motivational speaker, Mel Robbins, a study from the University of Calgary has revealed that around 85 to 90 per cent of students see themselves as procrastinators. But, as she argued at the 2018 North American Summit, '*You* are not a procrastinator. You have a *habit* of procrastinating.' And the reason for your bad habit is stress because putting off whatever it is you're supposed to be doing, *becoming distracted*, is an easy way to relieve emotional discomfort.

That stress might have everything to do with the task in hand. Maybe writing a business proposal for a group of interested investors is bringing up fears of failure. Or perhaps the creative side project you've wanted to crack on with has left you open to piss-taking from mates, as Louis and I experienced when starting ThruDark. *Is it any wonder getting started feels so bloody hard?* Outside factors such as health, finances, work and personal relationships might also cause you to spin out. So, rather than pressing ahead with the task in hand, you scroll through your phone, or spend the day working through a series of boring household chores. Anything to stop you from working on the one thing you should be doing.

The reason for this stalling tactic is self-protection. Your brain already feels under attack; performing a task it doesn't particularly want to do only adds to a growing sense of pressure. *Why not numb yourself by watching another show on Netflix?* But there is a way of breaking this destructive habit, argues Robbins. You only have to change the pattern, which she suggests doing in three ways:

1. Rather than dragging your heels about doing a grinding chore like your tax return, acknowledge the stress it brings. Trawling through your bank accounts is unpleasant, so don't pretend it isn't.

2. Halt your avoidant tendencies. Robbins suggests counting down from five to one as a way of short-circuiting the habit.

3. Work for a minimal amount of time. If you're struggling to get going in the gym, do five push-ups. If you need to work on an important presentation or speech, Robbins recommends writing for five minutes. Maybe there's a huge order of products to be picked and packed. Aim to dispatch five. Keep the workload short and sweet because research tells us that by simply getting the ball rolling, 80 per cent of people will press on and put a massive dent in their targets.

DEBRIEF

◆ Remember the *Compound Interest of Fucking Up*. Small habits can lead to big changes, good and bad, so cut the negative rituals out of your life.

◆ Recall your short-, medium- and long-term goals and establish a daily routine that will help you to achieve them.

◆ If you're struggling to stick to your positive daily routines, bring in an accountability partner to hold your feet to the fire if you fuck up.

PART THREE

IN UNION THERE'S STRENGTH

BRIEFING

Teamwork is a key element when serving with the military elite. It builds understanding, effectiveness and trust, and without it a group of operators will fall apart at the worst possible moment. It's for this reason that missions are planned in such a way that the effectiveness of the group is maximized, and why, when working on the ground, there's no place for selfish individuals or hotheads. Instead, there's a collective purpose in place and every operator in the line of fire knows that the others will have his back in rough times, as he has theirs.

Many people signing up for Selection get the wrong idea about its objectives. Yeah, it's about finding those students with the grit to withstand extreme pain while performing to an incredibly high standard. But the DS are looking for characters with the temperament to withstand those stressors while acting in the best interests of the collective. During the Hills Phase, for example, you can tell a lot about a person's true nature when they're absolutely chin-strapped. Negative traits, such as anger or defeatism, will always reveal themselves and when they do their impact can weaken the group psychologically. Any individuals displaying those characteristics are binned off fairly quickly.

It's not uncommon for a student to blow up in a moment of chaos – someone you might have previously thought of as being a next-level soldier. Under the horrific conditions, workload and fatigue they explode, or implode, and they're then marked down as being unfit for the job. Really, what the selectors are hoping to find is that rare individual: an incredibly strong character; someone who's quietly confident in their abilities and in possession of an acute understanding of teamwork, its dynamics and how it functions in high-pressure situations.

Once installed into the squadron, an operator soon learns about the ethos and values required to survive in what is a tight band of warriors. When I was badged, it was accepted that I'd have to match the exacting standards set by the group from the off, all while being constantly assessed by the people around me. (But I could also expect to see the same high standards in everyone else.) Elsewhere, the values of hardcore ownership, honesty and integrity were drilled into every serving asset and I learned why, on certain missions, the *most talented* person in the team wasn't necessarily the *right* person. At the same time, the brotherhood that grew in times of hardship showed me how teams should function and support one another, even in those moments when the gunfire had quietened down.

With the correct personalities in place, the specialized units within the UK Armed Forces have become a cohesive and incredibly powerful asset. The operators within these groups are aware of their roles and motivations. More importantly, they understand that the team comes first, the mission is everything, and it's important to put your life on the line for the people around you. The experience of serving with them has since shaped the way I view team building, community and the power of relationships in just about every aspect of my life. Now you can benefit from those same lessons.

11

NEVER ABOVE YOU. NEVER BELOW YOU. ALWAYS BESIDE YOU.

In the military elite there's a working code, an ethos that binds a group of operators together. This contract of written and unwritten rules, comprising the values of honesty, integrity, selflessness, force and strategy was important because everything we did in war was chaotic and unpredictable, and an intense level of trust, communication and support was vital for us to function.

In practice, this code was represented by the reassuring nod or hand gesture from a teammate as I prepared to step into a heavily guarded compound. It told me that somebody had my back. But there were other gestures that signified its presence, like the person who alerted me that my Bergen was unzipped when I embarked on a hard yomp over the Brecon Beacons, or the operator who shot an unseen gunman as I ran across an exposed stretch of battleground.

This concept makes for a particularly powerful force in business too, because people often want to cut corners and look after themselves rather than helping their colleagues towards a shared goal.

However, if a working group can commit to an ethos, or a list of shared values, they'll quickly realize that their chosen tools can yield impressive results…

Plenty has been written about the importance of unity when striving for success as part of a like-minded collective. At the highest levels of professional sport and elite industry, a universal sense of purpose and the desire to work hard for the people within the group can bring incredible successes. In the military elite, a shared ethos was the thread that kept our team of tier one operators together in some seriously grim moments. Among the lads I served with, this attitude created a feeling of inclusivity, as did the understanding that we were scrapping for a greater cause. There was also a sense of respect because everybody was considered to be the best of the best. Meanwhile, the group knew that the trust connecting us had taken a lifetime to earn, but that the bond could be torn apart without extreme dedication.

Before I go any further I'd like to point out that while an elite military ethos is often regarded as a mainly male construct (especially at the level I served at, which was dominated by blokes), for the purposes of this book and when shaping the identity of ThruDark, it's been long regarded as an all-inclusive term. The company takes great pride in the fact that we have men and women within our ranks. As far as I'm concerned, the ThruDark brand isn't about being male; it's about the connection with a similarly minded group of people of all stripes. Gender counts for nothing. Age, rank and experience are irrelevant too – and you don't get a badge for simply joining. You have to earn your spot.

There's no better mindset to have in place within a group of people than a shared ethos. (And we'll discuss how you can build one of your own in the coming chapters.) Though admittedly, the connection it created among the people I served with in war was pretty unique because we faced death every day, while running around, getting shot at and living the full range of combat stresses. Mates were killed; people experienced life-changing injuries. Those that were lucky enough to survive sometimes suffered from damaging mental trauma in the aftermath. In a war zone, the stakes were very high because if you were to fuck up at some level, there was every chance that either you, or someone alongside you, would die as a result. It doesn't get more nerve-wracking than that. And yet, I wouldn't have swapped those pressures for anything.

At the start of my service, I learned very quickly that it wasn't enough to have simply passed Selection, as impressive as that undoubtedly was. When signing up to a new ethos with the military elite I had to prove myself to the people I was fighting with, over and over again. I was told that respect would have to be earned and my past achievements counted for nothing. The upshot of this attitude was that I felt a constant pressure to perform to the highest standards, which was a good thing, and if I eased off for a second, someone would inevitably tell me about it. The other important realization was that friendships meant very little. Sure, I made some close mates in tier one service; there were also one or two lads that I couldn't stand, but all of that was forgotten during operations. The only thing that mattered was that everyone alongside me had my back, as I had theirs. As a result, the team ethos saved my life, and the lives of many others during war.

The attitudes instilled by the values of the military elite have since remained a constant in my life, thanks to the mates I do still keep in touch with. If I'm ever in a serious situation, I can call one of them in the middle of the night knowing they won't think twice about driving round to help. *But I'd do the same for them.* Thankfully, this has only happened to me on a few occasions, and I've made it through them all because the sensation of having a good *brother* to lean on wasn't dissimilar to those moments when I was creeping towards a compound door in the dark, preparing to step into the room, my weapon raised. The squeeze on my shoulder from my teammate in a terrifying situation told me that I was being supported. It said: 'I'm with you. I'm behind you. *Let's fucking do it.*' At no point did I need to look back to check that my arse was being covered. The security of *knowing* gave me the confidence to perform under extreme pressure.

Why am I telling you this? Because a shared ethos and a communal set of values can be an incredibly powerful factor in a group setting. It urges teammates to work harder for one another; individuals become selfless and diligent; episodes of slacking off or excuse-making are discouraged. An increased level of trust and respect develops; integrity and ownership is cultivated. And all the while, everyone works their arses off for a cause they've deemed to be much more important than any personal targets they might have set for themselves. (Though individual ambition shouldn't be curtailed too much.) Most importantly, nobody is left to struggle alone.

It might be that your business has stumbled upon a revolutionary idea within its field; your rugby team might be packed with star players and individual talents, but these resources can be wasted without a set of common values. However, by bringing in a shared ethos – the secret sauce – it's possible for that same group to surge towards an achievement that might have been considered out of their reach ordinarily.

* * *

The beauty of a moral code of conduct, like the one I was bound to in war, is that it can change from group to group, or institution to institution. Mine was obviously forged in battle, but yours, should you choose to create one – and I obviously recommend that you do – could be tailored for something entirely different. The most important thing is that the people working within your team clearly understand the unwritten contract and its values before committing to them with passion.

To achieve those values, it's important to define exactly what it is you're standing for in the first place. A team of mental health counsellors, for example, might define their ethos through the attributes of empathy, patience, flexibility, self-awareness and an ability to listen without judgement. (In many ways, this isn't dissimilar to the Hippocratic Oath, an ethical code taken on by people who work in the medical industry.) Elsewhere, bravery, community-minded spirit, a strong sense of discipline, people skills and the ability to thrive under pressure are characteristics that would be well suited to a job in the emergency services.

The values you select are entirely up to you, but they should be the principles that bring your team the most fulfilment. Luckily, there are plenty of options to choose from, among them: *Acceptance. Balance. Communication. Dignity. Enthusiasm. Family.*

Gratitude. Honour. Inquisitiveness… And so on. Once you've selected five principles that are essential to your way of life, the next stage is to put them into action. Yeah, scribbling a list of words down on a piece of paper and sticking them to the office fridge can make for a nice reminder on a day-to-day basis. But to ensure your values really take hold, it's important to bring them to every decision that you and your team makes, in the short, medium and long term.

I'm lucky. When it came to transferring a shared ethos to business, I'd already been schooled in the process because the idea was first introduced to me when I'd joined the Royal Marines Commandos. The values of courage (get out in front and do what's right), determination (never give up), unselfishness (team first; teammate second; self last) and cheerfulness in the face of adversity (make humour the heart of morale) were instilled in all the recruits through physical training and a series of repeated mantras at the barracks. Several years later, the elite military group I served with embraced attributes such as unity, honesty and integrity, and the relentless pursuit of excellence. Combined, this code created a strong identity for the people working within it and I realized that in many ways they weren't too dissimilar to a company brand. So when it came to establishing a set of values in business, Louis and I decided to stick to the same ideals…

FORCE: ThruDark has always worked with the concept of strength in mind, because we've had to punch upwards at times, especially given our size and budget when compared to the other players in our field. That hasn't stopped us from working hard and we've been uncompromising in our high standards when it comes to organization, design, production and marketing. From the outset, we've had a very clear sense of what the company should look and feel like: we were a tier one group; we were about the concept of endeavour through adversity; and we remained true to our vision. There was no way we were ever going to utter the words: 'You know what? Let's bow down to market pressure and make a purple jacket...' We weren't going to bend to fashion trends or fads if they didn't align with our vision.

STRATEGY: At the very beginning of our story, we often relied upon a 'cloak and dagger' mentality; we liked the idea of operating in the shadows – that was the MO of the units we'd scrapped with after all. It's for that reason that our identities weren't revealed in the early phases; we wanted to create a level of mystery. However, we realized that our individual characters were essential to the brand's story because they brought authenticity. When Louis and I eventually decided to reveal our identities, it was hoped that the people following our progress on social media would feel an immediate connection, as if they'd been part of something much bigger than the brand. *They were being let in on the secret.*

Elsewhere, we stretched our then small promotional budgets beyond what seemed feasible to create a series of hard-hitting, guerrilla-style promotional films. These widely shared videos, along with our outreach through a raft of ambassadors, created the illusion that we were an established company with some serious financial muscle, rather than a modest start-up. In many ways, this approach echoed some of the tactics first outlined by the Chinese military strategist and author of *The Art of War*, Sun Tzu: 'I will force the enemy to take our strength for weakness, and our weakness for strength, and thus will turn his strength into weakness.' People were often surprised when they were first presented with the reality of the company's size. The common reaction in the early days was: *You're only two blokes operating from a tiny office space?* Even now, with a team of around a dozen employees working under our umbrella, people fall for the idea that we're a much larger entity, but our aim has always been to appear bigger than we are.

HONESTY AND INTEGRITY: This idea runs across the brand in all manner of ways. From a production point of view, ThruDark wasn't financially positioned to use the ten best fabrics on the market in a style that we would have liked, so we chose the five strongest contenders, before running them across as many products as we could. *We wanted to make our kit as resilient as possible.* Throughout, we've always been upfront with our customers by alerting them to any issues or problems that might have delayed their order. We've also actively connected to our customer base by regularly informing them of any developments within the company. This has created a sense of loyalty between our target audience and the brand.

UNITY: From the off, we've attempted to build an atmosphere of unity and trust throughout ThruDark, by working, training and playing together. On a business level this has created a supportive atmosphere that binds the group – if someone's having a nightmare in one area or another, the others will rally around to provide reinforcements. Working out and suffering in the gym as a collective has also helped. As far as I'm concerned, this is a positive for the company. Endeavour through a shared sense of physical adversity often creates a tight bond among those people involved. It also fosters discipline, determination and dedication, traits I'm keen to see coursing through the business. Like the former England international rugby union player and current ThruDark ambassador, Dylan Hartley, once said: 'It's amazing how powerful training together is. When you have that collective accountability, the all-round energy levels, competitiveness and effort rises. Improved perform-ance naturally follows.'

Elsewhere, we've also given back to the people dear to us by supporting a series of groundbreaking expeditions. One of these featured Hari Budha Magar – a former Gurkha soldier who had lost both his legs in an IED attack in 2010. Hari was affected by post-traumatic stress disorder (PTSD) as a consequence. 'I am a soldier that's been trained to fight,' he said. 'In the past it was the enemy (I fought), but today… I fight to re-establish my mental health. I will live my life to the fullest whilst inspiring others.'

When Hari planned his attempt at becoming the first double above-the-knee amputee to climb Everest through his Conquering Dreams project, he approached a number of companies to produce a bespoke summit suit. None of them were able to do so. Recognizing his unique service and spirit, we stepped up and created a product specifically designed for Hari's needs.

THE RELENTLESS PURSUIT OF EXCELLENCE: Throughout Selection and during active service, I held on to the idea that I should work my hardest to up-skill and improve. I wasn't alone because at no point was an operator ever allowed to think, or act, as if they'd made it, or that they were the masters of their craft. As we rolled out of tours and into periods of domestic service, we were often sent on courses and encouraged to develop new techniques. As I've mentioned previously, in those rare days on tour whenever there was a lull in missions, most lads would visit a gym that had been built for us on base. At the highest level, there was really no such thing as a day off.

This search for perfection has since made up the backbone of ThruDark's business success. We've prided ourselves on being well drilled, overly prepared and expertly organized. When it comes to designing and manufacturing a new product, we assess every detail meticulously because we've worked to a long-held personal standard: *that'll do will never do*. The relentless pursuit of excellence has been ingrained into our shared ethos.

* * *

If your team follows your chosen collection of values with diligence, you'll be surprised at the improvements in performance and communication that take place. If you really crack it, the group might even move in a flow state, where everyone acts and reacts in perfect harmony according to the team's shared beliefs. This fluidity is often mentioned in sports like rugby and football where there's a well-worn cliché about players who form a strong connection on the pitch: *they're said to have connected telepathically*. But that's not true at all. When those two players had first met they would have been strangers. Having worked together tirelessly for hours and hours and hours, day after day, they've developed an understanding of how the other runs, or where he or she likes to position themselves. Usually there's a defining moment between them in training, or a game, *a click*, and from then on it becomes easy for the pair to read one another's actions. There's no psychic link though. Instead, a connection through their own ethos – in this case the scoring of goals, the success of the team and so on – has delivered incredible success.

It was exactly the same in battle. By training with the same group of operators, over and over, I knew exactly what the people around me were planning to do, often in the split seconds before they actually acted. I recognized micro mannerisms and subtle body movements that alerted me to whether an operator was going to move left or right, or to open fire or hold. Even in the dark it was possible to know who was around me, because I'd worked alongside my teammates so many times in the past that I could often recognize them by outline. As a result, we moved through rooms and compounds as one single, soundless, but functional entity.

It's possible for this same understanding to take place in a business setting, though admittedly it can be a constant work in progress. In every business space, there's usually a mixture of different communication styles and personalities. Some people are calm and considered; others are energetic and quick to flash in moments of confrontation. Everyone has their way of negotiating pressure, stressful situations, deadlines and heavy workloads. There are people who love to jump straight into a debate when asked about their opinions; others are more reserved and will wait to sound off, having decided they've needed some time to consider the question. It's important that when managing a diverse group of individuals that you come to understand the varied personalities in play and treat them accordingly. For example, during brainstorming meetings, encouragement should be given to the quieter members in the team; those louder, more dominant voices might benefit from a time limit in which they can speak. (One idea for organizing this conversational structure would be to have a playing card, or some other item on the desk. Whoever holds the card has the floor. Nobody is allowed to interrupt until that person's allotted time has concluded.)

Through trial and error, Louis and I have developed a greater understanding of one another through having committed to the company's ethos. We didn't physically work together in the military, though we knew of each other's reputation. In business, however, we've been able to build from our well-defined list of values, which have been important because in a highly pressurized environment, the potential for flashpoints can be quite high. Thankfully our connection and shared ideals have allowed us to handle those events effectively. Whenever we've locked heads, a frank, grown-up conversation has taken place in the aftermath. This process has generally made us even tighter, while strengthening the company's working practices going forward.

ACTION ON
Recruit with the Brotherhood Code in Mind

Selection isn't just about putting expert soldiers through their paces in order to see if they can cut it within the military elite. It's also about spotting those adept students with the characteristics to fit into a very unique group – people who show a willingness to accept the shared values of the elite units. When it comes to putting together any type of collective, it's important you follow the same blueprint. Creating a team of incredibly talented individuals with the perfect blend of skill sets is one thing. But if one or two of them have a toxic attitude – if they're lone wolves rather than team players, or unable to accept the cornerstones of your team's brand – then the working environment will sour very quickly.

The best way to do this is to check your installed values throughout the recruitment process. In the case of ThruDark, where force, strategy, honesty and integrity, unity and the relentless pursuit of excellence were key elements, we've always picked the candidates most aligned to those characteristics, and for the most part it's worked. Everyone has fitted neatly into our community (a concept we'll explore in the next chapter) and as a result, the team has regularly gone above and beyond for the cause. Meanwhile, nearly all the people we've brought in have remained with us for a long time. We even hired an industry expert from a leading brand in our market. When he made the decision to join us, his ex-employer called a meeting in a last-ditch attempt to retain his services.

'But I'm doing this because I want to work over at ThruDark,' he said. 'I think it's something really special and I want to be a part of it.'

That was just about the greatest tribute to our powerful working ethos I could imagine. Our new '*brother*' had realized that the unwritten rules in a company were just as important as an employment contract and he was being inspired by so much more than a pay cheque. If you follow the guidelines I've laid out here, you too can experience that same connection.

DEBRIEF

◆ Define your values. Pick five. Stick the list somewhere you can see it, and use them to inform every decision you make.

◆ Work, play and (positively) suffer together. A sense of shared endeavour through adversity will bring your group close.

◆ Once your values have been established, don't expect a flow state to happen overnight. Like a successful sporting, business or even songwriting partnership, connections take time and effort to strengthen.

12

CREATE COMMUNITY, NOT WORK

Defining your ethos and values is one thing. Encouraging a group of individuals to buy into it is another challenge altogether. But if you can create an environment in which every working member feels as if they're valued and respected, and fighting for a cause much greater than themselves, then this goal can be achieved more quickly.

One way in which the military elite achieves a strong collective mentality is by fostering a sense of community. The operators I served with respected one another. There was trust, a sense of ownership and shared purpose. We were a weird, dysfunctional family, full of misfits and fuck-ups, but we were a family all the same.

The upshot of these connections was that everyone scrapping in my team felt morally obliged to push through moments of pain and extreme pressure for the benefit of others. That in turn made us a more effective fighting force. But before I go any further, it's important to point out that community building is a tough job – a long list of sports coaches, politicians and business leaders will tell you that. However, by following some of the tips I've picked up in elite service, you might stumble across one or two ideas when galvanizing your group…

There were many ways in which community was forged in the military elite, though the foundations for supportive behaviour were usually laid down before Selection. A strong team ethic had to be present in every student if they were to pass through; loners and selfish types rarely made it towards the final phases of the course. Handily, this attitude was very much a part of my personality and I can remember stepping in to help those who were struggling around me during various stages of the course. I'd make a brew for the other lads when they were fucked. If someone looked physically ravaged, I'd offer to carry some of their kit, or cook for them once we'd arrived back at camp.

Because of my upbringing and the time spent with the Royal Marines, I understood that while we were a powerful unit of warriors, we were only as strong as our weakest operators, and pitching in to assist those in need ensured we would remain resolute when the going got really tough. But it was also a gesture that was being paid forward: by taking on an extra load for a lad in need, I hoped that the favour would be repaid when my turn to suffer inevitably came around. I wasn't the only one, and any lads who believed that this unwritten contract was beneath them – *the big egos* – quickly found that sympathy was in short supply when the shit hit *their* fan.

This attitude has proved equally important in the TV show, *SAS: Who Dares Wins*. In series five I was called in to work with Ant Middleton, Jason Fox, Mark 'Billy' Billingham and Melvyn Downes as 'The Mole', an undercover member of the DS who, for the first few days of filming, pretended to be a regular recruit. I worked with them, bunked down in the sleeping quarters and endured the same hardships as everybody else. Nobody had a clue who I was until my presence was revealed and it became my role to dish out the beastings. The one thing I noticed having played poacher *and* gamekeeper was the fact that the candidates who made it through to the final stages were those that understood the power of community. They didn't see the people around them as rivals. *They viewed them as reinforcements.* As a result they were able to lend support and feel supported, which made the group that much stronger. That meant the individuals within it were more likely to succeed.

All of us can benefit from this mindset. After all, none of us is an island; we're much more effective when we have assets around us to provide assistance. But building a community within a team of different characters can take time and serious effort. Luckily, I know of several sure-fire methods that will help you to get the process started…

CREATE PURPOSE

Purpose is the driving force in any community because with a shared cause behind you, one that's far greater than the individual, it's possible for your team to exceed expectations. While serving with the military my purpose was clearly defined: I liked the idea of testing myself in the toughest environments on earth and, sure, there was an element of wanting to keep my friends and family safe at home. I was also passionate when looking out for the blokes standing either side of me in a gunfight. As stated previously, I thrived on the idea of being an underdog and I wanted to prove to people that I could cut it with the best of them when the chips were down.

But a person's purpose can change through time and the things that drove me back then don't necessarily define me now. Yeah, I still want to test myself, whether that's physically, emotionally or at the company level. And of course, I want to look out for the people I'm working alongside in the office, or when climbing a mountain in the Himalayas. But these days there are other priorities, among them my wife and kids, the family home and one or two new endeavours such as jiu-jitsu. These are the things that bring me passion. And with passion, I rarely feel like I'm working, even when I'm up to my eyeballs in emails or kids' toys.

Purpose is a very individual concept though. It varies from person to person and for some individuals simply locating a source of inspiration can be tricky. But once you've found your calling, it'll propel you forward like rocket fuel. Having said that, it's not enough for your community to have only one person moving with passion. The whole group needs to be equally motivated, though not everyone within it will be driven by the same needs. For example, in an internet start-up, the CEO might have a burning desire to reshape the industry forever. The computer programmer could be inspired by new technology. The marketing director has a love for storytelling. While these motivational factors can be considered as being very different, it really won't matter if some harmony can be found between them. In this case, the CEO's ambition can be realized by the computer programmer's inspiring new ideas; the marketing director will be able to weave a compelling narrative about that connection as a way of exciting the marketplace.

Problems only arise when the entities within a community work at cross-purposes. That's when uncomfortable decisions have to be made about personnel and team structure.

VOLUNTEERING = UNITY

Altruism brings people close. Sacrifice tells everyone within a collective that whatever it is they're doing is more important than any product or customer service. But it also sends out a message to the participants. It says: *You're a team.* And as a result, what follows is a period of connection. *But why?* Well, in order to succeed in a charity drive, everyone involved undoubtedly has to endure some form of sacrifice, whether that's financial, physical or emotional. The only way to overcome these discomforts is for the entrants to band together, while providing support, strength and accountability. It's during these moments that community is built.

One cause close to my heart is mental health, because there are some pretty grim statistics flying around when it comes to the suicide rates among men in their twenties and thirties. At the time of writing this book, on average, around 125 people kill themselves every month in the UK, which is a horrifying number, and it's been reported men make up 75 per cent of that figure. Since retiring from the military I've done my best to support various mental health charities such as Rock2Recovery and CALM (Campaign Against Living Miserably) through physical and financial endeavours. But this was ratcheted up a notch when Louis's brother, Frankie Tinsley, decided to take on the UK's first ultra-triathlon for charity in 2021. Named Talisman Triathlon, Frankie's hope was that an arduous journey of 'effort, suffering, mindset, belief and sacrifice for a higher purpose' might encourage anyone on the brink to come forward for help.

If an ultra-triathlon sounds horrific, that's because it is. Frankie's aim was to cycle from Land's End to John O'Groats, before link-swimming the UK's longest lakes and running over the highest peaks in Wales, England and Scotland. He was determined to make it even harder by smashing through the challenge in just fourteen days. But Frankie had a very good reason for pushing himself so hard, which he'd detailed in a moving Instagram post when the project was launched:

'It was 9 January 2017 – I remember it because it was my birthday. I took a phone call to tell me that a good friend of ours had taken his own life. I thought back to the last time we had seen each other: three months earlier we had been out on a bike ride, after which, over a beer, we hatched a plan to establish a Great British Triathlon. The concept intended to deliver leadership and moral courage in the officer cadets that we were responsible for training. My thoughts on reliving that memory? *Now it's up to me to complete the event as a legacy to him.*

'Fast-forward four months and I shook hands with another friend. He was posted back to Scotland with his wife and his two-year-old daughter. We agreed to meet up next time I was in Scotland. Two days later, he took his own life. Subsequently we think he may have lost a battle with PTSD. I performed ceremonial duties at his funeral and I have a vivid memory of seeing my reflection in the funeral car as his coffin was unloaded and a Typhoon jet flew overhead in a sign of respect.

'One friend was brought up in Falmouth, Cornwall and the other was brought up in Ballachulish… I will link up the two families through this epic journey in their memory. By capturing their story and the inevitable hardship I will have to endure, I hope to help raise awareness surrounding suicide, promote strategies for a stronger body, mind and spirit, and support the charity CALM in their campaign to prevent suicide.'

As the Talisman Triathlon began, Frankie was very much up against it. He ruptured his appendix in training and ended up in hospital. But given the importance of ThruDark's ethos and values, both Louis and I – plus one or two others – stepped up to support the cause once Frankie had recovered. We ran, swam and cycled alongside him on various legs of the ultra-triathlon; Louis and I kitted him out in technical clothing and helped on the logistical side of the project; we promoted his cause online and produced special merchandise as he worked to raise as much awareness and funding for the cause as possible. In the end, Frankie completed the Talisman Challenge in fourteen days as he'd hoped, which was an unbelievable effort. He also managed to raise £26,000.

The psychological results of this event were mind-blowing. As Frankie raised money for a cause close to all our hearts, the unity within the participating group seemed to tighten. Every challenge or brush with adversity brought us closer. We grew as a team, and as the event wore on, it highlighted how self-sacrifice could bind a group of individuals. If you're looking for ideas to improve community in your team or company, think of a galvanizing event. Organize a collection drive. Enter into a collective fun run or sponsored hike. Donate clothing, money, even blood together. It might feel painful in the moment, but you'll be surprised at the unity it creates.

ARMOUR-PLATED OWNERSHIP

Ownership is a vital component in the community-building process and if fostered correctly it can create a powerful team ethic. Within the military elite, I learned that the ability to own my mistakes and flaws was one required of every operator. The person who can admit to a weakness is a person who can build on that weakness; a mistake that takes place in battle – such as a dropped map – needs to be acknowledged because that map might have handed some advantage to the enemy, but by having knowledge of the balls-up, we could tread extra carefully. Without it, we might have found ourselves on the receiving end of a grim surprise. There was an important caveat to all of this though: in the aftermath of failure it was important that the individual concerned worked on self-improvement because having a rogue operator that screwed up left, right and centre on a regular basis wasn't going to work for anyone.

I've been on training courses throughout my career where mistakes have been made, but people always 'fess up immediately. On some occasions, blokes have left equipment behind in their observation posts. In those situations, an operator understands that the mistake is going to result in a humiliating debrief. His reputation is going to take a dent, too. But rather than trying to style out the cock-up by heading back and retrieving their equipment (or making some desperate attempt at a cover-up), the people I've worked with have always radioed our HQ immediately.

'Stop, stop, I've had a nightmare,' they've said. 'I've left some kit behind…'

The mission then changes gear. We pause everything to pick up the kit and in the debrief that follows, the operator pulls no punches about his horrendous error.

The group accepts his honesty and he is able to move on as a result, but I can guarantee you he won't make the same mistake twice. For starters, our senior commanders wouldn't tolerate his presence in the group if he did. More importantly, by taking ownership, the operators in question preserve the spirit of our community. Despite the fact that they obviously let themselves down, the decision to act with integrity tended to echo with the ethos and values of our team. Yeah, people make mistakes (and pretty big ones sometimes), but they're still individuals we could trust, but only if they visibly upped their game.

In many ways, ownership, on both an individual and collective level, is the glue that holds a team together. It builds respect. It creates an honest environment. It establishes integrity. But it also encourages a collective to self-appraise without pulling any punches. That, in turn, allows for growth and improvement to take place. *But how can you apply it to your own life?* Well, for starters, you can be unflinchingly honest with yourself about your vulnerabilities and mistakes, as and when they happen. Don't cover them up. Don't bullshit. And don't blame others. But it's also about acting with due diligence. If you spot that the office printer has run out of ink, replace it. When an issue pops up at the end of a shift, stay late and solve the problem, rather than hoping someone else will take care of it for you. In times where you're feeling unable to cope, alert a colleague and ask for help before the situation becomes too severe.

These are the gestures that can develop unity and strength. If you're able to implement them correctly – and leading by example is always the best way – it's possible to create an almost addictive hunger for honesty. From there, a collective sense of ownership will sharpen your team while protecting it with a near-impenetrable layer of armour plating.

WIN TOGETHER; LOSE TOGETHER

When your group shares success and overcomes adversity it can create an incredibly rewarding environment in two ways:

1. By spreading the benefits of any achievements, you'll build an atmosphere in which each team member feels valued.
2. Collectives that can overcome errors or misfortune as a whole, without overly blaming anyone at fault, will create a supportive environment, especially if ownership has been embraced en masse.

Some successful companies use these tactics in a fairly basic way, but it's usually effective. For example, whenever there's an issue, they'll gather together to discuss the problem, without beasting anyone for making an honest, individual mistake. Then they move on. (It's a procedure that's worked well at ThruDark.) On the other end of the scale, during moments of victory, such as at the end of a healthy financial year, some companies deliver bonuses, dishing out a bit of extra cash to the team by way of a thank you for their efforts. They might have an end-of-year awards ceremony, or a regular moment of recognition for any outstanding individuals. (As I mentioned in Part Two, ThruDark has a jokey scroll that we hand out to our Employee of the Week. It's a piss-take really, but the underlying message is that hard work will be recognized and rewarded.)

Developing pride within a team is so important. I certainly felt it whenever I was serving with my squadron in combat. On those rare occasions where we were invited to an official function on base, and we arrived wearing our badges and berets, the lads from other regiments often looked at us with respect. That gave me a buzz. There was also a sense of honour within the collective. There were different teams within the UK Armed Forces top tiers and each one had a unique patch that was worn into battle. Among the iconography in my group was a badge of the *Marvel Comics* character Wolverine, who was an aggressive warrior. That in itself was an inspiring image. But I also wore a patch of the Union Flag to remind me who I was fighting for. (Not that I needed it.) These logos created a sense of honour; they were a sign of community, but they also built an inspiring rivalry among the different teams within our squadron. That competition pushed everyone to work that much harder. The communal successes we then experienced whenever a mission went well, or as a dangerous enemy was dispatched by our team, felt especially sweet as a result.

FAMILY IS AN ASSET

We still behave like chimps in many ways. For starters, we're pack animals; we have a collective mentality and we feel a deep-rooted desire for connection with the other people in our group. We crave acceptance; we fear rejection, and yeah, while some of us are OK with acting as lone wolves, the vast majority of people want to operate in a troop or tribe. The military elite understands this, which is why its squadrons are split into modest-sized groups – there's enough personnel to create a large fighting force with a tight connection between the individuals involved, but it's not so big that one individual could move through the crowd unnoticed, or unheard.

When I went to war, I knew everyone around me intimately. We spoke about our fears and goals, our successes and failures. We saw one another at our best and at our worst. Most of all, we heard about the loved ones at home, such as our partners, friends and families, and these connections brought us closer. Similarly there was a powerful bonding process that was taking place at home, thousands of miles away, as our other halves joined together via email, texts and meet-ups in a mutual support group.

This familial atmosphere really helped the lads on tour. We knew that our significant others were able to lean on mates that were going through a similar experience. They had friends that *understood*, rather than ones that didn't and who said things like: 'Oh, I don't know how you cope.' When tragedy struck, a caring support network rallied around the bereaved and when the lads came home, fit and healthy, everyone celebrated together. At times we felt like a massive tribe. After all, there weren't that many industries that required a person to say to his or her partner, 'All right, babe, I'm going to work now. See you in six or seven months… *hopefully*.'

Even though I'm not in the military any more, I behave in pretty much the same way. A friend of mine has just gone away on a tour of duty and our families have been very close for a while. The wives get on great and the kids love playing with one another, so while he's off, we'll make sure his family is looked after, which is a comfort for everyone. Over the years, I've come to learn that this attitude should extend to any group effort where a serious amount of commitment is required. My new career can be all-consuming at times. I know there are plenty of people out there who have a similar experience, and if the work in question is a passion, or important for one reason or another, then it's important the families of the people involved connect in some way or another.

That might sound weird, but when you're dedicated to a cause or project for significant chunks of time, or if your job provides you with an interesting community such as mine, then it can create a feeling of loneliness, or detachment, among the other people in your life. To counter any negative emotions, bring everyone together from time to time. Organize events where those individuals that are close to you (your partner, kids, friends) can meet with your teammates and their loved ones. That way everyone can connect.

On the face of it, this seems like an almost insignificant gesture, but the knock-on effects can be powerful. When work gets stressful, for example, or the commitment pulls you away from home, the understanding of what you do, why you do it and who you do it for can create a feeling of empathy. It also helps to head off any feelings of neglect or resentment. (Providing you're not spending *all* your time at the coalface, that is.) Furthermore, the friendships that form between the people outside of your working group – the partners, kids and friends of your teammates – can provide an emotional life raft in troubled times which we all need every now and then.

ACTION ON
Don't Be Jack

The doing of deeds, *and the people who do them*, often when no one else is looking, is what creates a functioning community. In the very literal sense it's the volunteer groups that pick up the litter at the weekend, or the Good Samaritans who collect clothes during charitable efforts. In the military, it was those individuals who cared for the whole squadron, either at the base or on the battlefield. Of course, there were people that didn't fit the mould, lads that were only out for themselves, and those characters eventually became pariahs over time. They even had a nickname. We referred to them as a *Jack*.

This term came from the Navy, as did many of the phrases in my line of work. Why, I'm not entirely sure, but during my time in the Royal Marines there were certainly one or two Jack types kicking around. They were commandos who would disappear while the rest of the team tidied the sleeping quarters before an inspection. They'd then make excuses for their vanishing act. The regular story was that they had somewhere more important to be – a meeting, a drill, some other activity. It was nearly always bollocks.

I remember working with one bloke who would fade into the background whenever the team came off an exercise and it would be our job to unload and then clear the artillery, vehicles and equipment. This was always a grim two- or three-hour shift and nobody really enjoyed it, but this one particular Jack individual always slipped away for thirty minutes at a time, leaving the rest of us with a much heavier workload. Before long, the other lads would notice.

'Where's Smudger?'

'Oh, he's gone to the NAAFI*...'

'What the fuck's he doing there?'

'He's getting a coffee...'

Jack-bastard.

To add insult to injury, whenever the bloke returned he would have only got a coffee for himself. At no point did he consider the wellbeing of his teammates.

In a community, such an individual can make for a toxic presence. Because of one bad apple, the collective will fail to reach their maximum potential. Resentment then builds among the other members (the people actually pulling their weight) and it's for this reason that – in the upper echelons of military service – behaviour like this wasn't tolerated. There was simply no time for Jack individuals, because the work was so intense we didn't have the luxury of being able to carry passengers. If anyone in the group displayed laziness, or a selfish mindset, they were jumped upon immediately.

Instead we needed our community to work with purpose, ownership and integrity. Anyone unable to fall in line had to be cut away. I suggest you adopt a similar tactic when building your community.

---

* Slang for Navy, Army and Air Force Institutes – a place where we could get hot drinks, snacks and so on.

DEBRIEF

- Community is a powerful bonding agent in any team. It shows the individuals that they're valued, respected and working for a cause greater than themselves.

- To build community in your group, make altruistic efforts together, arrange events that connect the family and friends of your teammates, and win and lose as a group.

- Don't be Jack. Do everything you can to avoid the reputation because it'll follow you around like a bad smell. If you spot one in your team, put them on notice.

13

PICK PEOPLE OVER TALENT

When it comes to the nitty-gritty of getting students through the Selection process, the DS aren't looking for the best marksmen, the fastest swimmers or the smartest strategists. (Though those qualities will obviously come into play.) Instead, they're seeking out resilient individuals with an armoury of skills and a malleable mindset; operators that are willing to learn and self-improve; characters that are equally effective when scrapping alone or when working as part of a team. Generally, the lads that make it into the top tier aren't the most talented people on paper, but they're undoubtedly the right people.

This criteria being in place is important for a number of reasons. Functioning in the theatre of combat is a stressful line of work. For the most part it's daunting, knackering and highly pressurized, and an operator will live in a state of fight or flight for long periods of time. That can be massively taxing on the nervous system, so it's no good being able to run 100 metres in ten seconds if you're the type of character that wilts when the going gets tough, which it always does.

By the same token, calm thought is very important, especially when trying to assess whether the car approaching your position is a civilian vehicle or a suicide bomber. It's for that reason that hotheads are usually weeded out on Selection. At the top end of military life, emotional control is everything, and hiring the right people for the job, rather than the most talented, can reap major rewards in the long run…

There's a very good reason why the military elite selects suitability over talent: *it's a battle-tested tactic for getting the job done.* Yet, outside of the UK Armed Forces, many organizations and industries put people to tasks on the basis of their seniority, or past achievements, rather than picking the person with the right attributes for a particular task. As a consequence, junior members of staff are sidelined, the newest face through the door doesn't always command quite the same level of respect as somebody with a decade of service, and the person down the pecking order (who might have a unique perspective on a given situation) is overlooked. I've learned that when square pegs are shoved into round holes like this, missions fail, and in the tier one units I served with, the right people were moved into action, regardless of experience or medals earned.

The importance of picking people over talent was really drummed home to me when I was part of a team that had been instructed to insert ourselves into a quiet fishing village in order to keep eyes on a mock target. It was a quiet place. The type of outpost where everybody knew everybody and outsiders drew inquisitive questions. This was particularly noticeable in the pub, of which there were only a couple, and our first job had been to arrive looking like the locals, before mingling subtly until we'd picked up the intelligence we required on our mark. In advance of the journey, we'd kitted ourselves in the type of gear that wouldn't have looked out of place on the TV drama *Doc Martin*. Think: tatty, heavy-knit roll neck sweaters, waders, wellies and beanie hats. Honestly, the level of detail and checks that went into our 'costumes' was incredible. Hair, beards and local style all had to be painstakingly applied to survive that first glance by a local in order not to compromise the mission.

We were on the back foot from the off. Not because we'd given ourselves away with a misplaced word, or a fucked-up cover story, but because the most senior member of the team was around six foot seven in height and built like a brick shithouse. When we walked into the boozer he stuck out like a sore thumb, causing the locals to turn around and gawp. Even the music seemed to stop, like it used to in the old Wild West films. As we ordered a round of beers I couldn't help but regret my decision to walk in alongside him.

'This is all sort of wrong,' I thought. 'Almost comical.'

Our cover was sure to be blown. Within a couple of hours we decided to pull back from the exercise area and a different team was reinserted.

I've experienced the reverse of this scenario, though. During another exercise at the start of my elite service I was tasked with working on a mock operation where an operator had to dress up as a homeless person in order to watch a person of interest in a major city centre. The task required some serious method acting. Our volunteered 'beggar' skipped the showers for a week or two because it was vital that he smelled and looked the part. Having filthy clothes, greasy hair and blackened fingernails was important. The look was then offset with a cardboard bed and a begging bowl.

For a few days, our spy hung out in shop doorways and on park benches in order to keep tabs on our chosen targets. On this occasion, the guy we'd selected very much suited the brief. He already had long hair and a beard. It also helped that his working-class, local accent meant that he didn't sound out of place on the streets. Had we chosen a bloke with styled hair, the perfect set of teeth and a plummy voice, he probably wouldn't have blended into the surroundings quite so easily if challenged. The funny thing was, the operator who landed that particular role was probably the least experienced member of the group and yet he carried the attributes to nail the job perfectly.

These were valuable lessons going forwards. During the business of mission planning, it was vital that the right people were generally selected for a task rather than the most skilled. And if that meant sidelining a highly decorated operator so be it: medals and time served didn't count for shit. And the more senior members of the team never grumbled or complained if they were given a backup role.

In many ways this structural organization closely mirrored that of jiu-jitsu. In the other martial arts – as in the regular army – you're graded by time. So, for example, in karate if you've been fighting with a certain belt for six months, you'll eventually earn the right to prove your skills and, if successful, advance to a higher level, or a different colour of belt altogether. That same process used to apply in the Royal Marines Commandos. (Though it's now a merit-based promotion system.) But in Brazilian jiu-jitsu, the grading system is completely different. *A promotion happens at the right time.* There's no structure, or order of events, and it doesn't matter if you've been 'rolling' at a certain grade for months on end. Instead, a fighter is put forward for their grading when it's been deemed that he or she is ready. That process could take six weeks, six months or even six years. It really doesn't matter, and the same spirit had been established in the military elite where operators were promoted on earned merit, rather than time served.

Or, at least, that's what's supposed to happen…

I was away on a six-month deployment when a troop sergeant returned to our fighting group. He'd been working in other positions for a while, outside of the collective. Meanwhile, I was a corporal having served for around four years and I was having an effective tour. We were smashing through a series of jobs and our success rate was high. The group had also formed a tight bond and team morale was strong, but when this guy joined with us (we'll call him Operator A) it became very clear that he was off the pace with the style of missions that were taking place. Because of his rank, he rightly assumed a position of authority,* but while he was undoubtedly a talented operator, he wasn't the right fit for the job at that time.

---

* Though the concept of rank doesn't count for as much in the military elite as it does elsewhere in the UK Armed Forces, a certain hierarchy has to exist in order for the group to function effectively. The last thing anyone wants is for a team of operators to be running around, doing their own thing.

Things went south pretty quickly. Operator A didn't gel with the team, and worse, he seemed out of touch with the tactics and techniques that were required in such a fast-moving conflict. Even the operational basics that were required of every serving individual seemed to be off. The rest of us were miles ahead because we'd been on the ground in recent months. We were dialled in to the latest weapons systems; we understood how the vehicles worked and how the unit should move when approaching a target from the ground. These upgrades were important in process because modern warfare constantly evolves and as the enemy adapted to our tactics, so we had to change in order to stay ahead of the game. There was no time to rest, and anyone missing out on those developments for extended periods would drop behind.

I could tell that Operator A was becoming increasingly uncomfortable at his lack of up-to-date experience. He would continually challenge the latest operating procedures and he didn't seem willing to learn from the younger lads in the group, even though they understood exactly what was expected of them. Rather than sitting back and listening to the resources around him, Operator A decided to enforce his outdated procedures. Whenever one of the other operators attempted to steer him in the right direction, his response was depressingly stubborn.

'No. We don't do it like that,' he'd snap. 'This is how it worked for me in the past, so that's how we're doing it. *I'm the troop sergeant.*'

The heated discussions nearly came to blows.

This situation was further evidence of why it's important to have a strict recruitment policy in your team or company, one that focuses on people rather than talent. When inviting applications for a job vacancy, a good way of executing this watertight assessment process is to look past the gold standard CVs. You'll be familiar with the kind of thing I'm talking about: the individual who seems too good to be true, a standout character with a great education, a well balanced portfolio of experience and an interesting career path. While these things are undoubtedly positive attributes, it helps to keep several things in mind when assessing who might be a good fit for the company:

1. Everybody upsells themselves on a CV. It's easy to blag and bullshit your way into an interview with a colourful document.

2. Always take a closer, almost forensic look at the covering letter. That's where the nuts and bolts of a person's personality can be found.

3. Scope out their social media footprint. Assess what type of person they really are.

4. Always consider credible, up-to-date references too.

Of course, this can present a risk in itself. *It might be that you overlook a real talent.* But by searching for the characteristics that suit your ethos and values, as established earlier, you'll have a greater chance of getting the perfect fit. It might be that your company is looking to fill a customer service position and one of the more unexpected applicants comes from an ex-trainee lawyer or journalist who's looking for a change of scene. Sure, they might seem overly qualified for the role at first, but look beyond the CV and check the covering letter. If there's something interesting about them, ask yourself how their unique skill sets might be utilized. For starters, both professions rely heavily on communication skills, so an individual with that background will undoubtedly come in handy when dealing with the public. Given their literary talents it might be that they can step in when writing press releases and PR memos. Or maybe they have an incredible passion for the business you're involved in.

It's worth noting that when the military elite assesses their students during Selection, they're not necessarily looking for the 100 per cent finished article. Yes, expertise is key. But at the same time, a potential operator with a willingness to learn and adapt is usually considered a much better option than an elite soldier with a stubborn attitude. Think like the DS; take a similar approach.

ACTION ON
Create Swim Lanes for Your Team

The military doesn't produce unthinking warriors at the elite level. They recruit skilled and determined individuals who can think on their feet and throw darts at the dartboard whenever a plan requires it. But beyond that, the personalities making up those units are varied and sometimes conflicting. There are introverts and extroverts; loud and quiet types; people who direct with words and those who deliver with actions. All those characteristics have a place in the group, but it's important to know how to prevent them from clashing. In war, the thread that kept us together was the reality that every operator needed the people around him if he was to stay alive. Bickering, egotism and rash behaviour could snap that thread pretty quickly.

In business it's often very different. People clash because the consequences for their actions are rarely fatal. The egotist who charges ahead with an unapproved deal (because he wants to make a point to his boss) won't have to step into a gunfight if everything goes wrong. He'll instead get a slap on the wrist for getting ahead of his station. This lack of physically dangerous consequences means that rifts and cliques can form, disputes happen and productivity slows. It can be a pain in the arse if a team is pulling against itself rather than moving forward as one.

A good way of circumventing this problem is for a company to create a swim lane policy. Or, in other words: to recognize the personalities within their team and then give them a space, or lane, in which to thrive. Team leaders should understand that it's important to watch over these lanes, in much the same way that a lifeguard controls the health and safety issues at the local pool. For example, if someone moves into the wrong area, it's vital the lifeguard heads off any problems by blowing their whistle. In the business sense, an individual getting in the way of another team member should be alerted.

For the most part, this tactic has worked well at ThruDark. There have been times when people in various departments have muscled in, uninvited, on the issues of marketing, social media and promotion. Unless they've been asked to throw darts in a team meeting, they're brought back into their lane quite quickly, and out of the path of any unnecessary collisions.

Elsewhere, we've worked out that the different departments within the company need to move at different speeds, and on those occasions when the whole group is required to make a collective effort on a particular task, their respective lanes are brought into consideration. For example, our social media guys move quickly; their work turns over rapidly; it's the nature of the beast. On the other hand, ThruDark's design and accounting staff operate methodically and with great care. When everybody comes together, it might be that the faster-moving swimmers can only pop in for an hour or two, before returning to their deadlines; the slower types have the bandwidth to dedicate larger, uninterrupted periods of time and so they're deployed accordingly.

The upshot? Understand your lanes and make them work for you. Then encourage your resources to swim.

DEBRIEF

- When building your team, use the available intelligence at your fingertips to assess any potential recruits. Look past the CVs, analyse the covering letters and check out their social media profiles in order to build a better picture of who they really are.

- Remember the gold standard candidate might not be the *right* candidate. During the interview process triple-check that a potential employee buys into your shared values and ethos.

- In the military elite, medals and time served counted for very little. So when assigning names to tasks, pick the person who you know will nail the job, rather than someone with the most experience, or years on the clock.

14

HIRE SMART, FIRE FAST

Selection for the UK Armed Forces' top tier is the job interview from hell – involving physical suffering and psychological turmoil that has upended some of the most resilient individuals I've ever met.

Throughout the course, anyone believing they can cut it at the sharp end of military life is scrutinized in a variety of environments and in all manner of horrendous situations.

Only the most resilient will make it through to the very end, which is why Selection is considered by many to be the ultimate military examination. But the process is extreme and painfully meticulous for one very good reason: only by hiring smart, and by testing every potential operator's limits to the max, is it possible to ensure that the right individuals make their way into the elite ranks. When it comes to putting together a team, this is a procedure that all of us can learn from...

I wasn't exactly 100 per cent ready for Selection when my chance came around, but as with most major life events, I knew the perfect moment didn't really exist. Still, my slight nervousness was understandable. Without telling me of his plans, a mate had loaded us both on to the summer programme, but rather than getting the hump about it, I figured, 'Why the hell not?' Before long, I was sitting in a room full of other hopefuls, unsure of what lay in store. Well, that's not totally accurate: I had a *vague* idea of what was coming down the track given I'd heard way too many horror stories, most of them from a long line of solid commandos that had failed to make the grade on previous Selections. My hunch was that in the short term there would be pain, and plenty of it.

On day one, I felt strong, and in many ways the experience wasn't too dissimilar to being on the start line of a marathon. My body was in peak condition. I was rested, well fed and injury-free. But over four weeks my body was broken by the grind of performing day-long yomps in the scorching heat, all while being weighed down by a heavy Bergen. Emotionally, the effort took an equally heavy toll and I found the regular monotony of navigating my way over a route with a map and compass – all the while worrying if I was on the right path or not – a real stress. With every day there were more and more questions. *Had I passed the time trial? Was I doing enough? Did I have it in me to finish?* I silenced the chatter as best I could by forgetting the past and ignoring the future. I could only concentrate on the present. I focused my attention at night by looking after my body, taping my swollen feet and squaring away my kit so that everything was ready for the next day. Self-care became my priority.

The military elite was a self-policing entity on the whole. The standards were high and anyone that failed to reach them had to be pulled up by the collective because a) there was a mortal risk in everything we did, and b) the success of any missions going forward depended on them. But during my Selection, it became apparent that there were one or two 'DS watchers' to manage – those thankfully rare individuals that slackened off during camp duties whenever the instructors weren't around, but who magically seemed to burst into life whenever they were. They were a demoralizing presence for any group grafting their arses off, and I realized it would be best for the military elite to tell the truth about who was shirking their responsibilities.

This wasn't snitching. My honest evaluation – and that of the other lads – ensured that no weak links would make it to the next stage. In many ways, it was one of the most vital aspects of the recruitment process because it weeded out the fakes, the individuals that liked the idea of joining with the most expert military squadron in the world, but who crumbled whenever the hard-core reality of special operations presented itself.

* * *

I was eventually ushered into a group of operators who would come to define my personal ethos and values. But more than anything, I came to appreciate the fact that the UK Selection process was just about the toughest entry exam in the world. It had to be, given the nature of the job, but even though I'd been brought into the top tier of operations on merit, the assessment process didn't end there. For a year, my peers and team leaders constantly checked my actions and behaviour. I knew that if I were to fuck up in any way, or if I pissed off the people around me too often, a return to the Royal Marines would have been on the cards. Even though the DS had decided I was absolutely deserving of my place in the team, I had to prove the extent of my abilities to the serving operators on a daily basis.

Because Selection was so intense, it was considered highly unlikely that an individual would pass the tests set for him and then struggle when the work began for real. No chances were taken though, and during my probation period, the Operating Commander received reports from everyone serving around me. There was no hiding place. Had I been unable to integrate myself quite quickly, or if I'd struggled to pick up the new skills and procedures, my flaws would have been pointed out. I'd have been told of the expected standards and what I needed to do in order to reach them. For the most part, when I did make a mistake, this process acted as an inspirational kick up the arse. But I also knew that if I really screwed up, my senior officers would hear about it immediately and their punishment would be swift.

This is a system that we've since introduced at ThruDark and we'll always give our new hires a period in which everyone can figure out whether we're a suitable match. One example of this took place when we first started the company. Louis and I had got it into our heads that we only wanted to work with people that were ex-military, in the belief that those individuals would understand our ethos and identity more clearly. This idea has shifted over time and we've realized that people from all walks of life can integrate into our practices. As discussed in the previous chapter, we needed specialist people for specialist roles, and their experience, or where they came from was secondary.

An example of exactly this type of character was our head designer. As the company took shape, we learned from Louis's initial recon mission to China (and the ill-fitting samples that were dispatched afterwards) that it would take some serious effort to arrive at the designs that would eventually launch ThruDark. Frustratingly, for the first few months we seemed unable to reach a technical clothing expert that we felt comfortable working with and the experience was disheartening. At that point we'd have been forgiven for abandoning our idea and giving up on the project, but I'd been presented with far tougher challenges in the past. Instead, I took the mindset that I wanted to be inspired.

We trawled Instagram for innovators, scrolling up and down, over and over, before we eventually stumbled across the British outerwear creative, Jeff Griffin. As a designer, Jeff shared the same independent values as we did. He prized authenticity over everything else. He was also madder than a box of frogs, which helped the relationship develop no end, though I was unsure of his approach when we first drove down to his eco retreat, Loveland Farm, for a getting-to-know-you meeting. When Jeff opened the door, he was wearing only one flip-flop. A dog then lolloped up beside him, an expensive-looking pair of glasses gripped in its jaws.

'What the fuck is going on here?' I thought, reminding myself that it wasn't the worst thing I'd seen dangling from a pet's mouth.

Jeff and ThruDark seemed intrinsically connected from the off. We certainly shared a lot of the same ideas on design, branding, core values and authenticity; we were honest about our inexperience and weaknesses, and the errors we'd made so far. When we told him our plans and what we were hoping to build, he became very excited. 'I like the passion in you two,' he said. There were doubts, though. While there was some capital behind us, in start-up terms it wasn't a limitless reservoir of cash and a creative of Jeff's calibre was unlikely to come cheap. As we travelled home, my mind considered the likelihood of us getting together. *Could it even be considered a meeting if somebody was only wearing one flip-flop?* According to Jeff, it very much could.

'Look, lads, I've had a think,' he said the next day. 'You've caught me at a good time here. I'm working with other people, but I'd like to help you out as a passion project.'

Jeff's 'passion project' took us to Milan in Italy where we met with textile factory owners and struck deals. As our probationary period began, the three of us turned our designs into samples and argued about stylistic tweaks and technical quality. There was a constant to and fro between how a jacket or a pair of trousers *looked* and how they *functioned*, and striking the balance between style and survivability – especially in a piece of clothing that was expected to operate at minus 40 or 50 degrees Celsius – felt like a never-ending battle, and one we weren't willing to compromise on. But throughout this process, the three of us gelled. Jeff came to understand that we wanted the DNA of tier one service to be entwined with that of ThruDark's. Having eventually achieved that harmony, it became clear that our first round of customers weren't that fussed about Jeff's flip-flops, or the fact that we'd taken a risk in hiring him because he wasn't ex-military. They just wanted to use the jacket.

This probation process was beneficial for both parties. In this case, we'd been able to figure out whether we wanted to work with Jeff, and vice versa. But really, this was a dialogue that could have been embraced in all kinds of team situations. I also realized that this style of assessment shouldn't be solely reserved for the newest people through the door, it should be an ongoing action, and we later made it a requirement at ThruDark that every individual filled out a self-appraisal questionnaire from time to time. In it, they had to rate themselves on a scale of one to ten across a variety of areas. We then drilled into their responses with a series of follow-up questions, among them:

What would you like to do to up-skill?
Where are your areas of weakness?
Where do you add most value?
Where do you see yourself in a year?

From there we established a personalized short-, medium- and long-term plan for each employee, setting out a series of targets that would both benefit them and the company. The results have only strengthened the ThruDark community. But if someone wasn't quite right, we've followed the standards set by the UK Armed Forces: *we've fired fast*. Unsuitable hires are as demoralizing in a business or organization as they are in a unit of soldiers, so we've tended not to keep them hanging around. Thankfully, this has happened to us rarely, and on the occasions we've had to part company with someone, we've done it in a style similar to the UK military elite: we've identified the problem and tackled the issue as quickly as possible by explaining the situation to the individual concerned and detailing our reasons for severing the contract. (While operating on the right side of employment law, of course.) We want everyone who leaves the family to do so with their heads held high. As with the military, just because someone isn't the right fit at the specialized level, it doesn't mean they're incapable of being an expert soldier elsewhere.

ACTION ON
Assess From All Angles

When introducing new members to your team or company, ensure that any toxic influences don't slip through the net by employing the same tricks that were used by the DS on Selection. By that I don't mean you should stalk your freshest employee as they perform their daily tasks, but there's no harm in gathering together a dossier of intelligence from the more established members of the group, by throwing around some questions. *How are they fitting in? Are they a team player? What are they like when we're not around?* From there you'll be able to paint a broader picture of what your new employee is really like.

One technique that is particularly effective when assessing your team is the 360-degree appraisal, in which everyone in the group takes time to anonymously grade the efforts of their teammates, and themselves. I remember hearing a great podcast featuring the owner of a famous British fitness brand, where he explained how he had even turned the spotlight on himself by getting his employees to each fill in a form in which they were asked to evaluate the performances of the company leaders. The results, when they came through, were sobering.

By all accounts, the company owner spent the best part of a week sulking about his assessment. He pored over the comments and numbers, and fumed over the negative viewpoints of his staff until, eventually, the issue was brought up by his partner at home. Having expected a reassuring ego massage over what he'd believed were clearly inaccurate reports, the owner was shocked when his other half offered a counter view. 'To be fair, that's a pretty spot-on analysis,' she said. The owner was forced to re-evaluate. Rather than letting the observations derail his work, he used them as a form of tactical analysis in two ways:

1. Instead of moaning about the flaws in his game (while patting himself on the back for any acknowledged strengths), he addressed the fact that he wasn't perfect, and that there were issues to deal with in the immediate future.

2. He listed the weaknesses and worked to improve on them. At the same time he drew up a list of his positive traits and figured out how they could be maximized in a manner that was beneficial to the company.

Sometimes it helps to view ourselves through the eyes of others. It's one of the many ways that the military elite bombproofs Selection and weeds out the DS watchers. But it's an invaluable tool in any team or business effort, where your group is only as strong as the weakest link. So find time to locate those vulnerable spots, whether they're in an employee, teammate or yourself – and work to fix them.

DEBRIEF

- Hire smart by assessing your new recruit over a chosen period of time. Ask the people working alongside them for their thoughts to ensure they're not a 'DS watcher'.

- Analyse your own performance by asking your employees or colleagues to fill in an assessment form that details your strengths and weaknesses. Swallow your ego and fix the flaws – we all have them.

- Be prepared to shift your position on the type of people you want in the team. The requirements of a group or project can change over time. Move with those changes, as we did when employing our 'non-military' head designer.

15

YOU CATCH MORE FLIES WITH HONEY THAN VINEGAR

All of us come into conflict from time to time: disputes with work colleagues, people in positions of authority and unreliable business contacts or deal makers. Any resulting flashpoints, if handled poorly, have the power to disrupt company-old connections, established supply lines and friendships, while massively disrupting procedures and plans.

Not unexpectedly, this reality was felt most keenly in war, where a lot of my work had the potential to be violently kinetic. But over a decade of military service I learned that diplomacy, or 'honey', sometimes applied through the subtlest of gestures, could prevent an outbreak of hostilities, whereas applying force, or 'vinegar', acted like a can of petrol on a bonfire. This tactic, as I would later discover, was equally applicable to industry, where it's usually best to think smart and sweet...

Door-kicking jobs were a stress and I never knew what might be awaiting me on the other side of the entrance. Sometimes we got lucky and the building was unguarded; on other occasions, the shooting kicked off immediately and the work would be hectic from then on.

In the frantic minutes following these operations, tensions were often frayed on both sides – nobody liked being shot at after all, and the bloody aftermath could be horrific.

During incidents of this kind the phrase, *'You'll catch more flies with honey than you will with vinegar,'* became applicable, and in many ways it echoed that famous adage about experienced football managers. Old-school sports leaders were renowned for getting results by expertly reading the dressing room: understanding which players required a boot up the arse after a defeat (the vinegar) and which ones were in need of an arm around the shoulder (the honey) could pay dividends. In the theatre of conflict, though, this understanding became especially prescient. Sometimes, in moments of danger, a local translator could freak out, or lose track of what was being yelled during a simmering argument with tribal leaders. Communicating with local police forces and newly trained soldiers could be frustrating too. Mistakes happened, missions got shit-canned. But shouting at a culpable teammate, or contact, rarely got us anywhere – especially if the language barrier was proving troublesome. Likewise, pretending that a problem didn't exist – *especially if we'd been the cause of the problem* – only worsened a situation further.

Instead it was much better to offer up a little honey.

This was best illustrated several years back, when I was working in a desert location. Night had closed in; the city was shutting down for the evening and the highway ahead was dark, but thankfully quiet – there was probably only a car or two around me. But as I approached a vehicle checkpoint, an armed guard stepped away from the cabin and waved me down.

'Oh shit,' I thought. 'I don't need this now...'

I shifted uncomfortably in my seat. Random checks at stages on the road were fairly standard and I guessed the guard would only ask me a few questions. Once he'd received the relevant information, I'd be sent on my way. Prior to moving into the region, I'd taken it upon myself to learn the local language. I wasn't fluent by any means, but I knew enough to make small talk, ask pertinent questions and follow a slow-moving conversation. Once deployed on the ground, I listened in to our interpreters as they worked and picked up even more phrases. I was able to wish good health upon a person and their family, and I knew how to talk to a stranger about their day without causing offence. While an education of this kind might have seemed inconsequential to outsiders, it was a valuable resource in times of high stress or conflict. Sure, I was authorized to use vinegar in moments of confrontation, but that meant employing force; I figured it much better to bring honey when attempting to de-escalate an argument or confrontation.

I would need jars of it at the checkpoint.

'As-Salaam-Alaikum,' I said to the guard, cheerily. I noticed he had two colleagues with him.

He gestured for my papers. His mood had darkened.

And that's when the dance started. I asked him how his day had been. He grunted. I told him about who I was and what I was doing. Then I told him to call his command to confirm I had the authorization to be driving at that time of night. But he wasn't having any of it. I started to sense an approaching flashpoint. Then he put his hand through a small gap in the window in an attempt to open the locked door. I grabbed his wrist to stop him, but he held fast and ordered me out of the car.

My heart sank. 'Oh shit,' I thought.

Sweat trailed down my back. When I then released my grip, the guard reached for his AK-47. This was not going well.

'Can I move on?' I asked hopefully.

'No.'

'Why not?'

'No, is why not,' said the guard. '*Out*.'

He looked towards the rear of the vehicle and my heart sank. There was stuff in there I really didn't want him to see.

'Wait—' I pleaded.

But the guard wasn't having any of it. He rattled at my locked door handle and shouted. Then he moved back a few steps and raised his weapon. *Why the hell has this guy gone from zero to a hundred miles an hour?* I couldn't figure it out. *Maybe my reluctance to obey orders had humiliated him in front of his colleagues? Perhaps the dude was a hothead?* I didn't have time to figure out the whys and wherefores of this particular power struggle. It was time to move fast.

I could have escalated the situation – the vinegar option – but I wasn't taking it. Simmering the heat of an argument was much harder when pistols were being waved around. Instead I opted for diplomacy.

'Hey, hey, hey,' I said, my hands raised. 'We can figure this out. I'm a friend... Hey, come on. *How are you?*'

The guard stepped back.

'Listen, we are on the same side,' I continued. 'Please calm down…'

I made sure to restrict my eye contact. As an experienced operator, I understood the issues that could arise with poor body language or overly aggressive glaring, especially when the language barrier was an issue. Turning away in frustration, or burning someone's retinas out with an aggressive stare could cause serious misunderstandings. I had been trained to talk in a calm and relaxed manner. I had to keep my hands steady too. And it was vital I looked away at certain moments, rather than eyeballing the guy for an entire conversation.

'Look, I can't get out of the vehicle,' I said. 'I'm sorry, I've got to move on. Please let me drive away.'

He rattled at the door again, though it was markedly less aggressively this time.

'Wait! Look—' I gestured to my phone on the dash.

'I'll make a call. I'll ring the commander of your security forces and put it on speaker phone so you can hear.'

The dude nodded and a gruff voice answered on the other end of the line. As we spoke, I watched the guard cautiously. When he was being spoken to, his demeanour seemed to change in a heartbeat. I wasn't fully sure of what was being said, but it sounded as if the commander was going to give the poor bloke a hiding if he didn't let me through. I was waved away in an instant, but I made sure to act with humility as I departed, just in case the pair of us crossed paths again.

'I wish good health upon your family,' I said, driving away, my heart banging, feeling thankful that nobody had been hurt.

I'd managed to neutralize my aggressor with kindness.

* * *

How we react to flashpoints can define the success of any project or objective. I remember a couple of years ago ThruDark released a jumper that Louis and I had been particularly proud of. It arrived with great material, cool branding and a unique seam of armour that had been woven into the elbows and forearms. The product went on an initial pre-sale and all 300 units were snapped up in a matter of days. We went into the Christmas holidays excited about where the new launch had taken us, while wondering how many more units we should produce in the new year. Then a troubling email landed.

'Hey guys, my jumper's broke. All the stitches are coming away at the elbows. This isn't working...'

At first we guessed the complaint was an anomaly. *One faulty jumper out of 300 wasn't bad.* Besides, a refund would settle the issue, or a replacement top when the next batch came in. But then another negative email arrived. And another. Before we knew it, over thirty complaints had been logged, and all of them were annoyed at what seemed to be a faulty fabric. Clearly we had a production issue on our hands and we had two approaches for settling it – the application of vinegar or honey. Using vinegar would have seen us sticking our heads in the sand. *Look, we've made the profit. Tell the customers we'll give them a discount on their next order.* But both Louis and I knew that such a position would have gone against everything we stood for, while signalling the end of ThruDark's reputation.

So we went for the honey instead.

Recalling all 300 units was a hugely expensive task and would have seen us financially hamstrung for months. *But really, what other option did we have?* We were a company that promised honesty, integrity and the relentless pursuit of excellence. Bailing on that MO would have destroyed our brand, so we sucked up the huge hit on our bank accounts and promised to refund or replace the product.

The results were instantaneous and overwhelmingly positive. The majority of customers happily accepted our offer of a new jumper. Very few asked for a refund *and* a replacement top. More importantly, those 300 customers understood we were a company that stuck to our core values, and the fact we'd opted for integrity over profit only amplified ThruDark's standing and enhanced our appeal. Our short-term financial hit was more than rewarded with long-term customer loyalty.

* * *

Opting for honey over vinegar when catching flies is a tactic we can all adopt – and quite easily too. This line of attack becomes especially powerful when working with staff, or operating as a team. Too often, people in positions of power bark orders to get what they want; they make demands, or come from a position of grumpy authority when really they'd be better served by asking for assistance and reframing their requests. For example, 'Can you help me with X...?' 'Can somebody assist me with Y...?' or 'Are you available tomorrow to do Z...?' works so much better than *do this, do that, and by this time.* Likewise, business exchanges – where communication is always essential – are better served with a deeper understanding of the person on the other end of the transaction or conversation.

For a greater handle on this, why not make a conscious effort to learn a few things about someone you might soon be meeting or trading with before you crack on with the work? Don't ask the basics and then move on (*How are you doing mate, all right?*). Instead, take an interest in *why* they're doing all right, or not. Find out what makes them tick. Check in on their family, football team, the music they're into. And remember these two rules:

1. Always listen for 75 per cent of the time and talk for the other 25 per cent, because it's better to gather intelligence than to give info away.

2. We all have two eyes, two ears and one mouth for a reason. Listen. Learn. And if in doubt, ask a question.

It might sound insignificant, but if the transactions or connections between you and the person you're communicating with begin to strain, you'll have a mutual understanding of one another, which in turn will create a fallback position from where you can rebuild. After all, it's much easier to sweeten a conflict with sugary goodness than it is with a bottle of Sarson's.

ACTION ON
The Power of Decorum

You can tell a lot about a person based on how they treat the service people around them – whether that's a waiter or waitress, the neighbourhood postie or an Uber driver. The one thing that drives me absolutely mad is when somebody disrespects an individual in that position. I dislike the way it makes the victim feel. I dislike that I have to see the scene unfold. I also dislike the lack of self-awareness in the person dishing out abuse. A truth we should all understand in life is that when money and power are stripped away, none of us are any *better* or more important than anyone else. So communicate with honey, not vinegar, and show some manners.

Acting with decorum is a powerful tool. An environment in which everybody treats their peers and colleagues with respect, no matter their position within the group, will buzz with productivity. Team morale will soar without resentment or office politicking; the component parts within a larger entity can move together harmoniously. If you're in a position of seniority, contribute to this mood by doing the small things for the people nearby: make a round of brews, buy the first beers in the pub, pick up one of the shittier jobs on the schedule when everyone else is feeling stressed out by the workload. Those actions will come back to help you when you're at a low.

Finally, if I've ever been in a spot where someone has annoyed me at work, or just in general, and I've been on the verge of reacting, it's been helpful to see the action from a different perspective – *theirs*. With that achieved it's sometimes possible to reach a level of empathy that's helped me to understand their attitude or actions and to alter my response accordingly.

Case in point: I was recently travelling through a busy airport at the end of a family holiday. The check-in line was huge. Everyone was jostling for position. Meanwhile, my kids were playing up and for some reason the bloke behind me would not give an inch of space. Every time I edged forward, even by a metre or so, I would hear a bang and a sigh at my back as he dropped his bag at my ankles. At times I could feel the dude's breath on my neck. On the first couple of occasions, I gave him a friendly glance to politely suggest that he was getting too close. It didn't work. After a few minutes of feeling seriously harassed, I was close to escalating the situation to an unpleasant level.

I'm more than aware that I can be quick to flash in a dispute. It's something I've been trying to work on over the years. But I've discovered that one way of calming my temper is to view a flashpoint scenario from the perspective of others. I took a deep breath and imagined some reasons for his unthinking behaviour. *Maybe the bloke was heading home to see a dying relative? Maybe he'd just lost his job? Or maybe he was just having a really shit day?* While it was highly unlikely that any of those exaggerated narratives were even remotely accurate, I knew that by finding some level of empathy I would do the right thing in a tense moment. I started to feel sorry for the bloke and my mood shifted. From there I was able to calmly ride out the pain of queuing, knowing I'd efficiently defused a time bomb in my head while sidestepping an embarrassing scene with a stranger.

DEBRIEF

- When applying honey over vinegar, remember that the little things count most: speak calmly, maintain eye contact (but don't stare) and keep your hand movements to a minimum.

- The trick to a successful conversation in stressful times is remembering the following numbers: listen for 75 per cent of the time, speak for the other 25 per cent. In times of conflict it's better to gather intelligence than give it away.

- When deciding whether to apply honey or vinegar, check your core values and imagine the end result of a messy dispute or some ill-judged behaviour. That should encourage you to take the sweeter approach.

PART FOUR

THE HARD LESSONS

BRIEFING

Following Selection, those individuals deemed expert enough to join with the elite were soon transformed into multi-faceted military assets. They jumped from planes; they jumped from helicopters; they jumped from boats. And all the while they had to perform to the highest standards imaginable – no slip-ups, no excuses. I found it incredibly intense work and it pushed everyone to breaking point, but I loved it.

When I wasn't fighting, I had to work hard in order to stay on top of my game and the attention to detail I had to put in was incredible. All the skills I developed, when combined, helped to transform me into an effective fighting asset, but they weren't born of top-secret techniques or hacks bestowed only upon those individuals with the courage to fight in the most dangerous war zones on earth. They were developed through characteristics present in everybody. For example, I'd realized that one of the key traits required in an elite level operator (in any field) was humility. It told me that I was nowhere close to being the finished article and I should do everything in my power to improve. I also learned from watching others fall flat on their face that ego was the most worrying adversary of all and I needed to defeat it.

Referring back to those lessons helped me to grow as an operator, and throughout my career there were teachable moments in communication, purpose and achievement. However, the most important truth of all was one that's been delivered for generations (though very few of us like to hear it): nothing is possible without hard graft. Life had taught me that from an early age, so when accepting the challenge of elite military service I knew all about the misery I'd have to endure in order to hit my targets. Likewise, I understood there would be periods of time where I'd feel utterly defeated, but I accepted those realities because I also realized that the qualities required to overcome any challenge were available to everyone. I only needed to know how and when to use them…

16

THE WHITE BELT MENTALITY

In martial arts the white belt is worn by beginners and it represents the first rung on a ladder that will take an individual to the top, or the rank of black belt. (Though the learning doesn't end there.) Regardless of their progression, the appropriate mindset of every karate or judo student is to act like a white belt at all times by soaking up every available drop of knowledge. Really, it's an attitude that everyone should be encouraged to embrace on a daily basis.

Why? Well, being in a position of constant learning – or the beginner's mind – does so much more than simply improve a person's skill sets. Rather, it keeps the wearer in a constant state of mindfulness because there's really no room for outside distractions. Added to that, it's also a smart operational play: to be in a constant phase of improvement allows an individual, or team, to stay one step ahead of the pack.

Similarly, in the military, operators are kept in a constant state of upgrade. The training bestowed upon everyone within the group is immense and, having passed through Selection, my learning was ramped up to an intense level. By the time I'd retired, a long list of qualifications had been added to my CV. To serve at the top tier I had to wear my white belt with enthusiasm, but the rewards were obvious...

Whenever an operator emerges from Selection, having undergone all that physical and emotional hell, it's easy to breathe a sigh of relief and to think: 'Well, that's the hard yards done. It should get easier from here...' *Welcome to mistake number one.* Because in truth the skills and techniques mastered were really only a taster for the work to come. Once passed into the military elite and badged, a new face will have arrived at the bottom of a very steep learning curve. My take: life with the top tier was not too dissimilar to a game of snakes and ladders, and passing Selection was like landing at the head of a cobra and sliding to the bottom of the board.

I can clearly remember the sensation of being a newly badged operator. I met up with my teammates for my first day of training and was sent to the stores so I could ready my kit. I really had no idea what was expected of me and the equipment on display was like nothing I'd used before. Everything felt alien.

What clothing am I supposed to wear?

What's my role in the group?

What do they want me to be carrying?

When I looked around me, I noticed the other lads were working intently, their heads down, carefully squaring away their own kit and admin. Meanwhile, I had a long list of questions and while I didn't want to be backwards in coming forwards, I knew that all eyes were upon me. I was the fresh face in a group of warriors. They were a brotherhood, overly familiar with one another's strengths and weaknesses, and my arrival was bound to come under scrutiny. I reckoned a lot of the guys would have been watching me closely, even though it didn't look like they were at the time. They were probably asking one or two questions of their own as well.

Who is this new bloke?

Is he good enough to serve alongside us?

What's going to happen when we throw him straight into the mixer?

In the end, someone took pity on me and explained exactly where we were going, the drills we'd be executing and the type of kit I'd be expected to bring. This marked the beginning of a mentally and physically draining chapter in my life in which I felt scrutinized to the max. Rather than wilting under the pressure, however, I knuckled down and adapted to my roles and responsibilities within the team. The work was gruelling and I can recall one or two training drills where a teammate literally grabbed me by the scruff of the neck and led me through a door-kicking operation while forcing me into the positions I needed to take up. *Walk here. Do this. Point your weapon there. Don't fuck up.* At times it was hard not to wonder if anything would ever click.

The only way to stop myself from becoming overwhelmed was to learn to love the experience. To do so, I adopted the White Belt Mentality, a psychological setting where everything about me was new, different and therefore a challenge to be mastered. (The opposite attitude was to give into the ego by wrestling with the experience and assuming that I knew better, or that I'd pick up the details later down the line, though that attitude wouldn't have impressed my peers.) Luckily, my personality was already dialled in to such a thought process and it was rare for me to lose heart if things didn't work out for me right away. Any failures I experienced were used as emotional fuel; they inspired me to work harder the next time. More importantly, I understood the learning process in my new role would be perpetual and personal growth was very much a part of the job.

This headspace also fed into some of the martial arts that I'd later take up when I eventually left the military. As I mentioned earlier, I was a huge Bruce Lee fan and had been introduced to Brazilian jiu-jitsu by a good friend of mine, Sam Sheriff – a former Royal Marines physical training instructor and the first ever Royal Marines black belt. Following on from twenty-two years in military service, Sam established the REORG charity's jiu-jitsu programme, which was designed to help former military veterans and first responders find balance in their mental health through intense physical exercise.

Taking up a new sport at the age of thirty-seven was a difficult decision to make. Despite everything I'd achieved in life, I would have to park my ego at the door, as I had done as a newly badged member of the military elite. Luckily, it didn't take long for me to rediscover my learning mojo and before long, jiu-jitsu was an important part of my daily life, as well as an incredible release after a stressful day. (Having someone fold your clothes for you, *while you're still wearing them*, is a great way to blow off steam.) The physical effort required to learn and succeed also became a meditative experience.

That might sound weird, but I've always been a bit of a hot-head, as evidenced by some of the scrapes I got myself into during my younger years. I could be short-tempered and aggressive. My usual release was to hit it hard in the gym; during boxing training, any frustrations I might have had were taken out on the bag. I later learned that going for a long run was a great way of clearing the mind, though I was sometimes easily distracted, and drawn back into whatever had been bothering me. But jiu-jitsu was mindful. To learn and progress, I had to clear my head and focus only on the moment and space around me. If I allowed myself to become bothered by outside influences, more often than not I'd have my arse kicked on the mat.

Most importantly, jiu-jitsu was a journey with twists and turns, and a skill that was nurtured over time. At the beginning, as a white belt, Sam told me I'd have to learn new techniques and disciplines in order to progress, and with every progression a stripe would be added to my belt. Once I'd added four stripes, I'd then advance to the next belt, and the next, until I eventually made it to the 'top' status: *the black belt*. Importantly, there was no road map to success and I didn't have a calendar or schedule to follow. To improve, all I had to do was focus, turn up and remain consistent.

With every new stripe I felt a rush of confidence, a reminder that I was growing, and the emotional charge reminded me of my days as a newly badged operator when I'd return from a training operation having successfully executed a task that might have previously tripped me up. Or when one of the lads patted me on the back after a mission and said: 'Nice one. You're smashing it.' With jiu-jitsu I found myself living in a constant state of learning and it was all-consuming. When I was rolling around the mat with my instructor, a guy called Nathan Johnstone, there was no time to worry about the boiler at home, or the latest office issue, not when I was 100 per cent on task. Even being pinned to the floor in an uncomfortable and humbling hold was a joy. It was in those painful moments that I truly learned about myself.

* * *

We can all apply the White Belt Mentality to our daily routines, personal endeavours and battle preparations, regardless of our age, experience and circumstance, and it's never too late to pick up a new skill or seek out a different experience. In fact, it's these moments that remind us of what our lives are all about. As a species we were designed to explore. It's the reason so many people have travelled to the ends of the earth, scaled mountains and crossed oceans: *to learn about what's on the other side.* The upshot of taking on the White Belt Mentality is that by accepting new challenges and placing ourselves under pressure, it's possible to grow and improve in everything we do.

Let me give you an example. During my time in the military I was promoted to the position of shooting instructor and ordered to train the attending teams on the range. The responsibility had been given to me because of my experience as a sniper, but regardless of my CV, there was a certain amount of pressure that arrived with such a position. Shooting was a life-saving skill. For much of our serving lives we were expected to hunt down bad people, all of whom wanted to do us some serious harm, so that meant the standards an individual was expected to reach on the shooting range were incredibly high. But the levels expected within an instructor were even higher. I guessed that standing in front of forty highly skilled operators while leading a close-quarters combat shooting course wouldn't be too dissimilar to having Gordon Ramsay watch while you made the Christmas dinner.

To deliver, I had to be confident; to get around my nerves I needed to become even more competent than before. (Because that's where the nuts and bolts of confidence can be found.) To achieve this emotional state I adopted the White Belt Mentality, even though the guys I'd be training already considered me a black belt in combat shooting. Sure, I could have taken a passive stance by simply *describing* the fundamentals of the course; nobody would have thrown a wobbly if I'd simply overseen the other lads as they followed my instructions – it's what a lot of people would have done in my position. *But that wasn't my way of doing things.* I wanted to lead by example, and so in advance of the course I spent hours, every day, shooting at the range. When the date of the presentation eventually arrived, I was able to deliver without too much stress.

This same attitude has been a constant at ThruDark. There really aren't that many days when the White Belt Mentality doesn't come into play, and Louis, myself and the other guys are forever researching new ways to improve the business because, really, it's the only way to maintain our position in the market. We've branded ourselves as leaders in the technical outerwear industry; our products have been forged in the heat of battle. If we were unable to keep up to date with the latest technological advancements in fabrics and tailoring, our reputation would fade pretty quickly.

To stay sharp, we read articles and books, and listen to podcasts. We've visited trade shows to see, touch and test the latest materials and fabrics. There have been meetings with business leaders, Zoom calls with business leaders and pub lunches with business leaders. In each encounter our intent has been to devour as much intelligence as we can lay our hands on. In our first year or so, we did everything we could to put ourselves in a position where we could eventually say: 'We actually know what we're doing.' At one point, Louis even enrolled himself on a business development course, as part of his leaving package from the military. He then completed a work placement in a clothing factory where he learned the finer details of how garments were stitched and pieced together.

As with the military's top tier, our education will never be done. It's worth noting that at no point does an operator reach a level where they can say, 'That's that. I've completed the learning.' Instead they're thrown into a series of courses designed to broaden their skill sets – in and out of combat. This same attitude is in place at ThruDark. Nobody has yet decided that our training is complete – and nor would they – because to be the elite you have to learn like the elite.

The best way to do that is by adopting the White Belt Mentality.

ACTION ON
Accept the Humbling

Becoming comfortable in uncomfortable situations is one of the beautiful skills a fighter can learn from jiu-jitsu and other martial arts, though it's rarely a pleasant experience. Being glued to the mat by your opponent can be humbling, especially when their knees are crushing your ribcage, and your limbs have been bent at a painful angle. However, if a fighter can breathe through the pain, all while retaining some semblance of calm, there's a small chance they might be able to escape. At the very least, they'll draw some new knowledge about their abilities from the encounter, such as the moves they failed to execute properly and the weak spots in their armour that need some maintenance.

A good humbling is something everyone should experience from time to time because there's always some value to be found in pain. Don't get me wrong: *it's horrible*. Nobody enjoys being humbled and the event can deliver an obvious blow to the ego. However, it's in these moments that everyone can learn something about their character, their strengths and weaknesses, and their emotional state. During my early days in the military, ThruDark and when scrapping in jiu-jitsu, I understood that every humbling – and there were loads of them – represented a learning moment. I worked hard to take advantage of them all.

The same can happen for you too. All that's needed is the courage to take on a new challenge, or to step outside your comfort zone. Learn a skill, or take up a different sport; push for a promotion, or launch a new product or venture. These events will place you under immense pressure at times and like a particular jiu-jitsu hold, you'll definitely experience some serious discomfort in the process. That said, if you can breathe through the pain, while assessing the mistakes that led you there, there's a good chance you'll emerge to fight another day, and with more knowledge and self-awareness than before.

DEBRIEF

- Adopt the White Belt Mentality: you'll learn new techniques, live in the moment and grow as a result. At no point does an elite operator think, 'That's it: I'm the finished article.'

- It's never too late to learn a new skill, or start a new adventure. Frighten yourself and take the first steps as soon as possible.

- Accept a humbling from time to time. There's knowledge to be found in pain.

17

EGO IS THE ENEMY

A fine line divides the benefits of confidence from the debilitating issues associated with egotism. In elite military service, carrying a strong sense of self-belief is vital when first applying for Selection, and then when operating in war. Without it, an operator can't make it away from the regular ranks and thrive as a tier one asset. However, in the thick of a mission, an ego problem can act as a death sentence. It encourages an individual to take risks, or to go it alone when their teammates need them to think coolly. Nobody wants to scrap alongside a soldier with a hero complex.

This same attitude applies in life, especially in actions that are team-specific. Chances are, you've worked alongside a character that tends to go rogue under pressure, or who thinks they know better than everyone else, and/or seems unwilling to listen to instructions. (There might have been a time when you've fallen prey to the ego and made the same mistakes.) The blowback when life inevitably turns sour as a consequence can be painful and humbling. However, by understanding the divide between assured action and a big head, it's possible to walk the line with comfort…

During my third year as a Commando I joined up for a sniper course. At the time, I'd been giving some serious thought to signing up for Selection but I'd deliberately kept those plans to myself. It turned out that one of the instructors on the course had the same idea, though he was being much less discreet about it and was claiming that he was using his time teaching us as a 'beat up' before the real business of Selection began. He shot his mouth off whenever he could. He acted the bully and came across as a real prick. Sadly, I found myself crossing his path in the foulest of circumstances.

We'd been moving across Woodbury Common, staking out a mock enemy target. As I crawled slowly and methodically through the gorse and into an opening of exposed ground, my sniper bag behind me, I spotted a divot ahead. It was only a small dip in the terrain, but I figured it might provide me with some modicum of cover. But having edged towards it, it seemed the instructor had spotted my intentions too. He stepped out of the undergrowth, unzipping his trousers as he walked, and pissed on to the floor, laughing to his watching mates who were observing from the gorse. When he finished his business and walked away, it felt like I'd been screwed. The divot was filled with his rank-smelling liquid. If I walked away in anger I'd fail the course; if I crawled around the divot, it would mean taking the wrong line, and I'd also fail the course. I had to suck up the rage and crawl into the puddle doing my best to ignore the warm, ripe liquid splashing about my face and arms.

But I'd soon get my own back.

Not six months later we were both on the Hills Phase, running through a series of gruelling time trials on the Brecon Beacons. I prided myself on being physically fit and fancied my chances of doing OK. And when I saw the instructor from my sniping course – the same arsehole that had pissed in front of me – I was reminded of another interesting facet of the Selection process. Among the students, rank counted for nothing. Everybody was set on an equal footing.

'What the fuck are you doing here?' he snapped, having spotted me on the first day.

I laughed. I didn't need to take his shit any more. 'What the fuck are *you* doing here?' I responded.

The look on his face was a picture. The realization that he wasn't in a position to push me around had landed. *And he wasn't pleased.*

When the work started for real, it didn't take long for the recruits to drop away like flies. I'd been placed on a summer Selection and the weather was brutally hot. Lads blacked out; others struggled to keep up with the required times needed to pass and failed the course. But through a combination of fitness and sheer bloody-minded determination, I was able to hang in there, passing a particularly hot time trial with only one other recruit. Everybody else had failed to keep up, including my old instructor. When I crossed the finishing line I noticed him cooling off in a nearby stream. He eyed me nervously.

'Have you just passed that?' he said.

Yeah, I did.

I then rubbed his nose in it by revealing my final time, and he fumed. Within days, he was binned off the Hills Phase and sent packing to his regiment under the guise of an injury, or some other Mickey Mouse excuse. Revenge was sweet, but it had also been educational: pride came before a fall. Shooting your mouth off could lead to trouble.

I would remember that lesson with every success at ThruDark. As we've gathered momentum, there have been times where I might have been excused for getting ahead of myself. At the beginning, I knew that making bold proclamations, or shooting my mouth off to mates in the pub, was a rookie trap – I've known a lot of people that have stumbled into it when leaving the military. Later, as we've maximized our bold ideas and unleashed huge amounts of potential there have been times when Louis or I might have become overly excited and bolshie, especially when we've smashed our targets in the face of some challenging global events. Instead we've decided to maintain a sense of humility, a psychological position that was drilled into us during war.

This is a mentality I enjoy because I've always liked the idea of being the underdog, and I've become determined to maintain a similarly understated position, even when things are going great. I don't want to make enemies or set myself up for a fall and I believe that ThruDark's results should do the talking for me. It's an ideal I've tried my best to stick to. Also, hotheads and loudmouths often make bad decisions on the battlefield; those same bad decisions can end in serious injury or death, and I've witnessed at close hand how a cocky attitude can result in humiliating failure. I don't want to repeat those same mistakes.

* * *

Carrying an ego into conflict is a big problem – both at an individual level and within a group. At a larger scale it can cause a fighting force to underestimate their enemy. For centuries, ragtag armies have thrived in harsh environments; they're well equipped to survive the climate and able to turn the harsh landscape into a tactical advantage. A number of invading armies have wrongly predicted that they can take over without too much trouble. *We're superior military. Nobody can keep up with us. We're the best fighters – the fittest, the strongest and the fastest. We'll just stroll in and do our thing.* Sadly, it doesn't quite work out that way and the so-called inferior forces have won out in the end.

An ego problem can also create just as many problems at an individual level, and, as a consequence, can cause a whole unit to function at a standard that's considered to be way below their optimum. If one person decides they're better than the others within their group and begins acting the hero, rash decisions can be made and morale can falter. Plans fall apart and lives are sometimes lost in the chaos. That's why a strong character and the ability to work well within a team are highly regarded qualities in the military's top tier, and why bad personalities are usually weeded out by the Selection process – either as a direct consequence of their attitude, or indirectly, as evidenced by my old sniping instructor on Brecon Beacons.

During Selection, rather than bigging myself up, or banging on about the fact I was having a (rare) good day, I reminded myself of the hard work that had brought me to that point and the effort required to move forward even further. Beyond that I made sure to remain disciplined in everything I did until the job was done. I later extended this spirit to my life after war. As

ThruDark has grown in size we've decided that operating without ego is an ethos that we are determined to instil within our working team, especially after the lessons we'd learned through tier one service. Rather than lording it over the new recruits working the warehouse, or swanning around the place with our chests puffed out, Louis and I have thrown ourselves into the dirty work. Given our senior positions inside the company, nobody would have minded if we'd operated from our offices and only involved ourselves in the high priority stuff – we'd earned the right after all. *But fuck that.* We made a point of mucking in on the 'shop floor', picking and packing orders as they've arrived. We've dealt with customer queries and swept up the workspace. And when things go wrong, we've coughed up to our mistakes rather than shifting the blame on to someone else. We've wanted to set a positive example from the off.

Sadly, that attitude doesn't play out in a lot of commercial companies. Having worked in that world for a short amount of time, I've noticed that there are plenty of people who seem to be working for one person only – themselves. They don't give a shit about how they arrive at where they want to be, or the people they tread upon to get there. *It's all about them.* Yeah, that attitude might work out in the short term, but over the long haul it tends to cause problems. Like those selfish recruits on Selection, the lads who are reluctant to help out whenever the chips are down, they soon discover that their actions have consequences. The business types that always impress me are those individuals who understand their role as a piston in a highly functional engine. Their lack of ego helps the overall group to survive and thrive.

That's the ethos I've always wanted to work towards.

ACTION ON
Leave Your Ego at the Door

The ego hates to be schooled. It despises the fact that a setback – a failure, dispute or some stroke of bad luck – can diminish its sense of self, or reduce its reputation within a group of people. Following on from a humiliating episode, it wants to lash out, or to react in such a way that the slighted person feels better about what might have been a shitty turn of events. (Usually at the expense of someone else.) But those responses are often dangerous: they can turn a bad situation into a catastrophic one very quickly.

The bottom line is that everyone is affected by ego in some way or another, and to a certain degree, age and experience can amplify the problem. If you're successful in your field, the ego might tell you that you've learned enough, or that your achievements in X, Y and Z mean it's not important that you listen to advice from a younger voice, or develop new skills. But that's a fast track to failure and if you can instead control the ego's debilitating influence and accept new lessons, or muck in with others who possess less experience than yourself, it's possible to absorb the cock-ups whenever they happen. From there you can become stronger, both as an individual and as a team player.

This became most apparent to me having spent a few years serving with the military elite. I'd watch experienced Marines with ten or fifteen years of expert soldiering under their belts join *our world*. They might have completed a couple of scrapping tours abroad, or worked as mountain leaders – they were clearly competent; they had experience; and having passed through

Selection it had been confirmed they were able to operate at the highest levels. After joining up with their squadron they'd be expected to work with new faces, new kit and new routines. There was no hiding place. A fresh face would have to hit the ground running and learn their lessons on the fly.

The operators that succeeded were willing to learn. They worked in a quietly confident fashion and were able to adapt to their new environment; they functioned as part of the team and understood their role as that piston within a highly functional engine. By leaving their egos at the door and understanding there was still plenty to learn, they absorbed the hard blows when they arrived. But for those lads unable to keep their egos in check, the problems would kick in straightaway.

For the most part, *The Big I Ams* were weeded out during Selection, but any (rare) bad apples that had slipped through the net were exposed in the first weeks alongside their new teammates. I used to be able to spot them from a mile away. They'd arrive and shoot their mouths off like there was something to prove; one or two of them might have bragged about having a really high pass on Selection and everything about them screamed: *Check. Me. Out.* By the time they'd screwed up for the first time on dive training, the established lads in the group would have brought them down to earth and reminded them of the reality of elite military life. Often, these reminders were fairly blunt. New operators not matching the high standards of the group were told to sort themselves out, and if they couldn't they should 'fuck off'.

'Fucking sort it out,' someone would shout. 'What you think you know isn't relevant. You need to relearn and re-understand how we operate and what we're doing. *Now.*'

Those operators that wouldn't, or couldn't, change, often reacted badly because their personalities weren't able to handle the humbling. In some cases they'd be pushed back to their relevant units. But sometimes a cocksure lad on the end of a verbal beasting would thrive in the aftermath. They'd park their ego and crack on. Then they'd grow to be more effective than they ever were before. And the others around them improved as a result because the weakest link had been reinforced.

DEBRIEF

- Egos are a big problem in any project or mission. At the group level they can cause conflict; within the individual they can breed serious character flaws including complacency, rash decision-making and aggression.

- Prove yourself as a team player in your group by mucking in with the dirty work – even when you're not expected to.

- Prove your worth with deeds not words. Remember: pride usually comes before a fall.

18

KINETIC INTELLIGENCE IS A WEAPON

One of the most important lessons to be drawn from the military elite is the way in which we utilize information and assess our personal performances. We're particularly proactive in this area because in a kinetic war, where the action moves at an often breakneck and sometimes daunting pace, it's important that a fighting force re-evaluates their position every now and then, rather than stubbornly pressing ahead with the initial plan. In the military elite, these moments were referred to as either hot debriefs or Quick Battle Orders (QBOs), and we used them to assess our resources while evaluating the changing situation on the ground. From there we'd make a judgement call on what to do next.

A hot debrief was completed as quickly as possible after a mission had been concluded; in moments of chaos we relied upon QBOs, usually as a reaction to some unexpected development – both good and bad – or the collection of new intelligence. I've held meetings on the back of helicopters, in irrigation ditches (while taking cover from enemy fire), and when hunkered down in the desert during an airstrike. Our on-the-hoof discussions were rarely quiet intervals of self-reflection.

Elsewhere, hot debriefs and QBOs are also an essential tool in everyday life, where plans can just as easily turn to shit. I've found that rather than pressing ahead with a schedule or mission, it's often better to prevent an inevitable collision with disaster by taking some time to regroup. From there it's possible to sketch out a new tactic. It's also true that taking a second to pause can help anyone to view a problem from a different angle. So remember: the hot debrief/QBO is an asset in times of crisis. If the military elite can lean into them during a war, there's really no reason why you can't too...

In conflict, a stubborn attitude to operational decision-making can turn a bad situation into a horrendous one. There were one or two occasions when I came under fire from a village that had been presumed safe. Rather than carrying on with the initial mission as instructed, it made sense to halt and conduct a hot debrief, or QBO. In those situations a series of questions were asked in order to paint a clearer picture of what was happening:

Is everyone OK?

Where did the attack come from exactly?

Do we have enough numbers to mount a sustained assault?

Once our circumstances had been judged, the big decisions on whether to retreat, attack on foot, or call in a more tactical strike were made.

I've found that the same attitude can be applied to other high stress events. Say, for example, you're about to pitch your company's services to a potential trading partner. In the minutes leading up to the presentation, it's discovered that a rival company has promised to undercut your fee at a slightly lower rate. The mood among your team changes in a heartbeat, everyone feels deflated, and though it might seem as if you're powerless, you've actually been presented with two options – stick or twist. To stick is to think, '*Fuck it. We'll press ahead with the original offer.*' To twist is to call a hot debrief and turn the intelligence to your advantage. *Maybe there's some wriggle room in which you can undercut the lowball offer? Or the smartest move might be to call off the meeting in a tactical retreat?* Either way, you've regained some semblance of control.

During my previous line of work, the hot debrief/QBO helped me to execute a number of incredibly dangerous missions. This happened even when a detailed plan had been laid out beforehand with all the intelligence and resources available to us. There were times when I've crept up to a building as ground commander, or as the lead convoy commander, where simply driving towards our final target was high risk because the roads we were travelling were considered to be some of the most dangerous in the world. In those situations it was important to remain focused. My senses always heightened massively; moving around discreetly carried its own challenges, and yeah, we usually had the cover of darkness as our ally, but any sound could travel far and wide. Even as our vehicle doors were quietly closed on missions I always felt acutely aware of our proximity to the target. In those moments, my concentration levels and senses were set to Condition Orange.*

---

* In military terms, this is a series of phases we use to describe battle preparedness. They run as follows: Condition White: We are unaware and unprepared; Condition Yellow: We are in a state of relaxed alertness; Condition Orange: We observe a potential threat; Condition Red: The threat is real.

When things went wrong on high-pressure missions, there was little time for messing about. I knew that in the time it took to regroup after a mistake or issue, one or two enemy fighters might gather their senses enough to fight back. Moving quickly was the key and I always called a QBO with my teammates. It was the only way to transform a chaotic situation into an organized plan because, without one, the missions would descend into anarchy. Luckily, I was always able to turn these situations of chaos around and a botched approach or entry to a mission was transformed into something positive. My training always played a key role, though whether I'd have achieved similar results by stumbling forward blindly, without a QBO was unlikely.

There are a few rules to consider when running through a hot debrief or QBO:

1. DO IT FAST

There's really no point messing around, mainly because perspectives can change with time and people will forget the important details. Our hot debriefs and QBOs were always conducted on the ground and in the moment where possible. If a mission had gone horribly wrong, the meeting was called as soon as we were back at the base. Getting all the details while they were fresh in someone's mind was incredibly important, especially on the kind of operations we were dealing with because even the smallest detail could unlock a key piece of intelligence.

EXAMPLE: Your business has experienced a major dispute between a client and a member of staff. It's an ugly scene. The client accuses your colleague of inappropriate language and rudeness; your employee reacts by calling the client a liar. In the aftermath it's important you get all the details down as quickly as possible while it's fresh in everyone's memories.

2. GET A 360-DEGREE PERSPECTIVE

On a fast-moving mission, every operator has different roles and different perspectives. With all these different jobs taking place at once in such a high-pressure scenario, every member of the working team will see the operation from a different vantage point. If a balls-up does happen and a hot debrief, or QBO, has to take place, getting the views of everyone on the ground will help a team leader to gather a clearer understanding of exactly what's happened.

EXAMPLE: In the aforementioned employee–client dispute, make sure to ask everyone around the situation for their take on what actually happened. *What did they see? What did they hear? Were there any other relevant details they might have noticed?* In this case, the client might have been incredibly aggressive in their language *before* the flashpoint took place. It might have been that nobody heard the offensive language that was alleged to have been used. With a 360-degree perspective, it's possible to get a more rounded take on a fast-moving situation.

3. IGNORE HEARSAY AND OPINION

We all interpret things differently and our memories can be influenced by other factors, such as hearsay and opinion. I've been on missions where I've sworn blind that something has happened, but someone else has seen it differently. For example, that we paused briefly due to a grenade exploding nearby. Then, in the same hot debrief, a teammate will claim the sound of the grenade popping off was actually some incredibly loud gunfire, or an airstrike nearby. In chaotic attacks, things can easily get confused.

EXAMPLE: When taking into account the intelligence you've gathered in the workplace dispute, filter out the external influences before making your final call. Don't listen to gossip. Ignore anything that's being posted on social media. Deal with the situation by examining the relevant intelligence that was gathered immediately after the event rather than anything you might have heard later down the line. Then make a decision accordingly.

In the fallout to a scrappy mission, where things hadn't gone entirely to plan, it was important to follow those three points so we could figure out exactly what had gone right, and what had gone horribly wrong. The first stage was to figure out what had actually taken place, and the operators involved discussed both what they'd seen and experienced, and the feedback always proved to be very telling. Usually, I would come away understanding why mistakes had been made, and certain incidents caused me to plan my future missions very differently from then on. In military terms, lessons of this kind were referred to as Post Op Appraisals and this collected information was then used to plan similar missions going forward. As far as I was concerned, they were invaluable sources of information.

* * *

Sometimes intelligence gathering could be a slow and methodical process too. When I was a sniper with the Royal Marines Commandos, every marksman carried a small notepad with them for reference. Known as a DOPE Book (Data On Previous Engagements), it would be packed with information gathered from the shooting range – real-time intelligence on what happened to the rifle and its ammunition in various climates and altitudes and in all manner of weather conditions. With every session at the range, I would draw together a greater understanding of the terminal ballistics – and external ballistics with real world data – while recording every nuance and detail as it happened. This then came in handy when the shooting started for real. Unlike a kinetic operation where the action was very fast-moving, a sniper and his partner would often have time to stalk, watch and then assess the best course of action before pulling the trigger. The DOPE Book was a vital resource.

In many ways, a manual of this kind was similar to the type of details carried by a professional golf caddie. Anyone unfamiliar with the trade probably assumes that these people are nothing more than a well-paid bag carrier, but in reality they're highly skilled and technically aware. On the eve of every competition it's the caddie's job to mark the course, measure the greens and gain an understanding of how the course should be played. When competition time comes around and their golfer stands over his or her ball – anywhere on the course – the caddie will know the exact yardage to the target, the speed of the wind and the best club to play for that particular shot.

I've been on many jobs when I've leaned upon the DOPE Book for assistance. I might have been perched up in an elevated mountainous position, with my target moving half a kilometre away. Rather than simply firing and hoping for the best, I'd use the equipment I carried with me to measure my altitude, plus the temperature and density air pressure. Then I'd flick through the DOPE Book, all the while asking questions and looking for pointers from a time on the range when I might have fired from a similar position. Without it I would have been relying on guesswork, which was never a good thing to do.

The DOPE Book has proved to be a vital tool in business too, where I've found that data can be fed into important future decisions regarding process and performance. For example, imagine that you run a product-orientated company, like ThruDark. It could be that you make bags, underwear or even beer. In these industries there can be a lot of moving parts when it comes to the introduction of new product lines, or even when restocking familiar items. Sometimes the decision-making process can feel a little overwhelming. However, if you've kept a DOPE Book to chart your previous strategies and their subsequent results, a lot of the guesswork can be taken out of those decisions, and in all the key areas:

DESIGN: How long did it take you to design the product? How much did it cost? What designs work best for the market? And how many stages did the company have to go through before the new product was signed off?

PRODUCTION: How many months generally make up the manufacturing process and at what expense? Is there a similar item in the DOPE Book that might make for a good sale comparison? If so, how many units should you make? Adjust the quantity and sizes accordingly.

SIGN OFF: Who calls the shots on signing off on the product? Is it a lengthy process? If you're not happy with the product, what happens next – and at what cost?

DISTRIBUTION: How many units go where and to whom? Which outlets sell your items in the biggest quantities? What's the best way to handle any surplus stock?

MARKETING: How can we utilize our data-driven research and analysis of consumer buying habits? What targeted email and social media campaigns should we run?

These are intimidating decisions, especially when you're leaning into guesstimates and hunches, and as I've explicitly told you: *hope is not a plan.* So commit to maintaining a DOPE Book because data is king and a steadfast resource for when making educated choices in potentially overwhelming situations.

ACTION ON
You Can Drop Your Sword in Battle, But You Can Never Drop Your Shield

Throughout my military career, I learned that the way in which a force defended was sometimes as destructive as their offensive resources. This wasn't exactly a new concept. Whenever the ancient Greek army attacked as a phalanx, the lead centurions would often raise their shields in front of them as a defensive wall. The individuals behind them were then ordered to lift theirs above their head to create a protective roof. This rudimentary barrier covered the warriors below as they were bombarded with arrows, rocks and other projectiles. As the force moved forward, the lead soldiers were then able to attack any oncoming assailants with their spears and swords.

Interestingly, the strength of this armoured battalion was found in its defensive elements, not its weapons: if one of the centurions were to drop their sword as they moved, it wouldn't really matter. The other weapons around them would still work just as well. However, if one of the soldiers was to drop their shield, the once impenetrable wall could be breached and the battalion would become compromised.

There's a lot that can be learned from both the modern and historical equivalent of this tactic. In life, we often forget about defending the cracks in our armour as we press ahead with an idea or project. We might be financially exposed in some way, or our personal relationships run the risk of becoming strained because of an increase in commitment and workload. Maybe our health is under threat, or we're unable to find the time to look after ourselves with exercise and good nutrition. If these weaknesses aren't tended to, our plans will fall apart, no matter how powerful our talents, or weapons, might be.

In business, the shield that has protected me the most is the brotherhood within ThruDark. I've been lucky enough to work in a team where everyone has pulled together for the benefit of the group. Everyone works to the best of their ability and looks out for the other people around them. If one person drops the ball or makes a mistake, the team will work even harder to keep the unit strong. So far, our metaphorical shields have remained raised through some tough times; the enemy hasn't been able to get in.

Meanwhile, there are other shields that keep me strong outside of work – my family, my friends, my commitment to physical exercise and personal challenge. All of these things combined have helped me to stay strong and improve as a person. So figure out your shields in life and make sure to nurture them. Keep them raised. For as long as they stand firm, you'll find the hard road much easier to travel as you head for home.

DEBRIEF

◆ In times of chaos, fall into a QBO. Gather your team together and establish a clear picture of the unfolding events. Then rethink your next course of action.

◆ Remember the three rules of a QBO: 1) Do it fast. 2) Get a 360-degree perspective. 3) Ignore any hearsay and opinion.

◆ For the major decisions in your business / project, note down your actions and results in a DOPE Book. This will give you a data-driven understanding of how you should react when faced with a similar situation.

19

MEDALS ARE FOR MOTHERS: THE SUCCESS CONUNDRUM

As I said in a previous chapter, it's been claimed by the military elite that 'Respect is earned through deeds; that medals are for mothers to admire and our real enemy is the oldest enemy of all – ego.' In other words, the silver and fabric awards we received as a result of our efforts were ultimately worthless and potentially dangerous – a warrior that leant on his past successes was highly likely to become distracted, or worse, complacent. There was simply no room for that attitude in my former line of work.

In war, this attitude is clearly defined. To slacken off is to hand the advantage to the enemy, and who knows what horrific events might take place as a result? In a business and personal development sense, this attitude makes for a healthy safety check too. A high achiever can easily fall by the wayside, having been made lazy by their recent results.

However, there is a simple workaround to this problem. I've discovered first-hand that it helps to reimagine success and recognition as a layer of psychological body armour. By forgetting the awards and focusing on the steps and hard work that helped to attain them, it's possible to become bulletproof to future failure…

In 2014, I was training out of the country, when a voicemail pinged on my phone. It was from my regimental sergeant major.

'Staz, the big boss is trying to call you,' he said. 'I know you're away, but this is very important.'

My mind zipped through a hard drive of worst-case scenarios.

Was everything OK at home?

Had something kicked off abroad and I was being called back into action?

And then, typically: *What the fuck have I done wrong?*

The reality, when I spoke to the commanding officer, came as a pleasant surprise. I'd been written up for the Conspicuous Gallantry Cross, a medal that was handed out for courageous acts in the theatre of battle, and second only to the Victoria Cross in terms of combat gallantry awards. At the time of writing this book, around sixty individuals have received it. Being awarded one felt like a massive honour.

My role in two major incidents had seen me put forward, as detailed in a commendation letter:

> His extraordinary performance throughout his tour, and in particular his courage, initiative and inspiring leadership during two events averted at least two major attacks and saved many lives. At this stage of the campaign a successful, high-profile terrorist attack would have had crippling consequences. For this he is absolutely deserving of national recognition.

As far as I was concerned, the events I'd been involved in were part and parcel of the job. I certainly wasn't imagining recognition or glory when I'd performed them, though I definitely went above and beyond what was expected of me. On both occasions, I'd been trained to win out, but I had to push through the fear to get there. But at the same time, the work had felt exhilarating. I was living on the edge and in many ways being so close to death – as was the case on both jobs – had made me feel alive.

The presentation ceremony was held at Windsor Castle and attended by none other than the Queen. As she pinned the medal to my chest, talking to Her Majesty was all a bit weird, like an out-of-body experience, and a nervy commentary raced through my mind. 'I can't believe it. *It's the Queen!* She's standing two feet away from me, shaking my hand. Now she's talking to me… *She knows what I did to get here.*' Having been instructed to speak only when spoken to, I responded in my poshest telephone voice – the kind most people adopt if ever they're required to chat to a vicar. The seconds passed by like minutes. My mind drifted as if I were floating away in a weird bubble.

The buzz didn't last long and I was back to work a day or two later, with nothing in the way of fuss or fanfare. The night before the ceremony I'd enjoyed a meal with the family and stayed in a nice hotel, but other than that there was no need to celebrate or get drunk on success. I hated the thought of going overboard and if anything, I experienced the psychological drag of imposter syndrome: I wondered what the other lads would make of my success and whether they considered me deserving of the award. I settled myself by remembering that I'd been celebrated for all the right reasons and my reputation in the team had been pretty solid in the past and so it would remain. I was right, too. Within an hour or so of rejoining everyone on tour, after the congrats and the questions, my accolades were forgotten. The rhythm of war began again.

* * *

Success generally affects a person in one of two ways. On one hand it can serve as a motivating force and a benchmark of personal standards. On the other, it builds the seductive narrative that an individual has made it; that they're better than the people working around them, or they've earned the right to ease up. I was lucky. In the aftermath of being told I was about to receive the Conspicuous Gallantry Cross I ignored the seductive voice. I sensed it might lead to arrogance, or that my performances and working relationships could potentially suffer as a result. Rather than psychologically 'wearing' my medal, I boxed it away as a benchmark and the Conspicuous Gallantry Cross* became a bar to aim at whenever high standards were required, which they always were. *I wanted to remain elite.*

I had witnessed the consequences of what could happen to a person when they walked around with a big head, especially during Selection when one or two lads who had been considered to be bloody good soldiers in their units arrived with an attitude problem. To their way of thinking, there was little doubt that

_____

* The fact that I'm actually discussing some of the successes of ThruDark in a book might suggest that I'm flashing my medals. I'd counter that by saying I'm using them as illustrative case studies that might help you in your personal missions.

they were making it into the military elite and they wanted to alert everyone around them to the fact. Selection, as you'll know by now, was a humbling experience; it was impossible to pass through without some level of humility. The lads chained to their previous successes, *their medals*, were usually the first to drop out.

This weeding process ensured that any successful candidates entering into the military elite were doers, not talkers. They were operators that didn't need to brag about their achievements, or big up their future successes – they got on with the job instead. This would be my mentality once I'd eventually returned to base following on from my Conspicuous Gallantry Cross award. One or two mates came up to me and congratulated me. Some of the new faces wanted to chat about the scrapes that had led to my nomination. Overall, though, the mood was one of acceptance. There was an understanding that everyone in my shoes would have behaved in exactly the same way, I just happened to be in the right place at the right time and if anything, the medal was a badge of honour for the whole group. It represented the fact that we were thriving at war's sharp point, which gave any aspiring soldiers, individuals with their hopes set on specialized service, something to strive for.

Nevertheless, the pressure to succeed was instantly amplified. At times, I sensed my teammates were watching me. Not in a way that was negative, or judgemental, but I felt an expectation to perform at a higher standard and as a result I wanted to prove that my accolade hadn't been a one-off. I didn't want to let anyone down. There was no hiding place either and not much later I was promoted to the role of chief sniper instructor, which was another prestigious accolade hanging around my neck. It was also a title that brought an extra level of pressure, and if ever I doubted my ability to succeed, I'd use the psychological accolades from my past to shove me forward. I unboxed the medal in my head and used it as a cue, one that told me I could deliver.

This attitude was a mental trick you can use too. It isn't exclusive military practice, or some psychological hack created by the Armed Forces elite. To master it, you really only have to compartmentalize your wins as they happen and recall them as motivational tools in times of trouble. The trick is to enjoy the moment as it unfolds before boxing it away. For example, it might be that you've picked up an annual award, enjoyed a massive creative success or seen your revolutionary organizational ideas implemented across the business. In those moments, sure, enjoy the celebration… *But then hide the accolades away.* Because it's depressingly common to watch the Employee of the Month blow their gains having allowed success to go to their head. Instead, think of your achievements as armour: when adversity strikes or a challenge needs to be tackled, they can act as a reminder of the times in which you've previously succeeded. (If it helps, write down a list of all your lifetime achievements – big and small – and then put them in an envelope somewhere. Go to them when you need a boost.)

I used this same technique having left the military, though there was one caveat: when it came to the mechanics of starting a technical clothing company, neither Louis nor I actually had any relevant medals to fall back on, other than our military experience and credibility. *But that was enough.* The creation and management of ThruDark was likely to throw up a number of stressful challenges, with scary consequences for both of us, and while we weren't yet hotshots when it came to nailing presentations or strategizing delivery schedules, the honours we'd both picked up in war reminded us that it was possible to manage pressure and function effectively under stress.

For example, I had a family to care for. Packing up a well-paid job with the military was considered a massive financial risk and, at first, I struggled emotionally, especially once the security of a monthly pay cheque had been stripped away. For long periods I was living hand to mouth while the company got off the ground. Whenever a payment trickled in, there seemed to be a never-ending list of financial outgoings, and at times the pressure threatened to become overwhelming. But it was during those moments where I'd remind myself of the mental hurdles I'd successfully overcome in the past.

When mentally reframed, the strain of meeting the mortgage repayments was really no different to the strain experienced when passing through Selection, or scrapping it out in a gunfight. Sure, the stakes were different. *Nobody was going to die if ThruDark failed.* So it helped to remember that stress was an emotional response; the psychological sensations when facing down a massive credit card debt was no different to the one experienced while working through a mission or training exercise. If that sounds weird, remember: emotional discomfort is still emotional discomfort whether you're maxed out on three credit cards or crawling on your hands and knees in rough terrain. I'd handled crushing stress before and so I'd handle it again, by reminding myself of my achievements in those moments when quitting might have been a comfortable option. I was able to push through the mental turbulence freely from then on.

ACTION ON
Treat Success as a Booby Trap

Being successful is a rush. It feels great. However, it's in moments of glory that we tend to let our guard down. As Denzel Washington told Will Smith following his controversial Oscars meltdown in 2022 (in which he'd slapped the comedian Chris Rock onstage and picked up the award for Best Actor), it helps to remember that: 'In your highest moments, be careful; that's when the devil comes for you.' I'd been trained in the military to remain on high alert once a mission was executed effectively, because there was every chance that the enemy might strike back. If that was the case, and we'd been shaking hands and backslapping one another rather than focusing on the job in hand, any advantages we might have gained would have been wiped from the board.

In moments where I'd been successful, I've tended to fall back on the discipline and techniques that got me a shot at victory in the first place. I knew that, yeah, I had to feel some pride in whatever it was I'd achieved at the time, but I wasn't going to allow any positive results to cloud my judgement in the future. I also knew that I had to work with humility and respect. This step was performed in two ways:

1. GO BACK TO THE DARTBOARD

Any honours I'd received in service, or any successes I might have made with ThruDark, were an integral part of my personal growth, but I viewed them as battles won. As in war, I understood there would be many more scraps to come, so I would immediately prepare for them by taking some time to throw more darts at the dartboard. (As outlined in Part One: Battle Prep.) This was done in five stages:

1. I'd check the board by constructing a new plan, something that would inspire or challenge me in the coming months or even years.

2. I'd see if there were any new darts to throw. These would be skills that I'd recently developed, or wanted to pick up in the future.

3. Make failure fun: I'd enjoy the process of learning from my mistakes; I'd seek out feedback on what I was doing right and what I was getting wrong. Every screw-up was viewed as an opportunity to grow.

4. I wouldn't overthink the failures. I'd feel the sting of frustration, draw the lesson from whatever I'd done wrong and move on quickly.

5. I'd stay focused, by not comparing my dart throwing to anyone else around me – or the team, if it was a collective effort.

2. KILL THE NEAREST CROCODILE

Louis and I have often been spun out by the emerging threats around us. On the battlefield, those issues – or crocodiles as we've come to name them – could be fatal. In business they've carried the potential to derail us creatively, financially or logistically. The medals we'd picked up in service showed us that we had the mindset to select our targets effectively, no matter where we were working, or in what industry. The skill when you're being attacked from all angles is to understand which crocodile to kill first. This was particularly pressing in the aftermath of a victory where it would be very easy to become distracted or complacent.

During those moments of potential weakness, we've always steadied ourselves by immediately establishing our most pressing issues. These were referred to as the closest crocodiles, and we'd work out how to tackle them most effectively. That might sound obvious, but so many people fail to address their tasks on a daily basis. They talk, speculate, criticize and put things off to the last minute. They scrabble to pay their tax bill on 31 January rather than putting money aside throughout the year (if they run their own business). They'll chat for thirty minutes at the start of the day rather than working through the overnight emails. And they'll leave the exercise they hate the most until the end of their training session, rather than squaring it away in the first ten minutes.

Once we'd established our most pressing crocodile, we would then set out a plan of attack so we could neutralize it. On some occasions, that might be as simple as sending out an email or making a phone call. But more often than not the challenge was more significant. On those occasions, we'd work backwards from the ideal outcome by setting out the key events that had to be executed in order to get us there.

The new jacket is a success – do we have enough in stock? Can the suppliers get the numbers to us for the product launch date?

Can we get the designs to the manufacturer by the deadline?
Do we have a key product in mind and what features would we like it to include?
New season, new product range – what do we want to do?

The final step in dealing with the crocodiles swimming about us was to have a series of regular briefing sessions where the most pressing challenges were addressed, names were put to tasks and deadlines were established. At ThruDark we have a meeting first thing on Monday to look at the week as a whole. This is followed up by a series of daily meetings, or GBOs, so we can check on how everything is progressing. By figuring out our biggest crocodiles we're able to avoid any unpleasant ambushes.

DEBRIEF

◆ Emotionally box away your successes. Refer to them as benchmarks to aim for whenever you have to operate to a high standard. (Which should be always.)

◆ Use your success as fuel. Show the people around you that it wasn't a one-off and inspire your teammates with discipline and diligence.

◆ In moments of doubt, return to the psychological medal cabinet and remind yourself of those previous victories. You've done it before, so you can do it again.

THE FINAL WORD

THE HARD ROAD WILL TAKE YOU HOME

In most books the pep talk arrives in the opening pages. It tells you to find purpose, or to prepare yourself for the grim yards ahead. While these sentiments are admirable (and usually spot on), by the time you've come to the last page and absorbed the lessons inside, the most important takeaway of all has disappeared. The one that says: You're going to have to work bloody hard to succeed.

Think of this chapter as that motivational talk. Throughout the book I've given you the tools to battle prep and the techniques, tactics and procedures to strategize like an elite operator. I've explained how teamwork is utilized at the sharp end of war and outlined some of the hard lessons that have helped me to thrive in moments of extreme pressure. However, without the willingness to push through the inevitable moments of serious discomfort, it's unlikely those tools will work as effectively as you would like.

This final lesson will help you to rationalize the experience of suffering. It won't act as a painkiller, or magic away the physical and *emotional agony, but it should give you just enough encouragement to see your challenge through to the end...*

All of us should have a mantra that encourages us to work harder. Yours might come from a book, the lyric of a song or even a film. Maybe it's a line from a famous explorer or Stoic, or something more personal, such as a saying from a loved one. Mine came from the colonel (Introduction: Endeavour Through Adversity) and the speech he'd delivered to my squadron in the Bottom Field during my time on Royal Marines basic training. *The hard road will take you home.* Whatever you choose, take the words to heart. Pick apart what they really mean to you. Then, whenever life feels challenging, remind yourself of the mantra, over and over. If you're in the gym and you're about to crack through twenty dead lifts, don't fall short. Use your inspiration to stop yourself from quitting at dead lift number eighteen, because dropping two reps means taking the easy road, and by doing so you'll fail in your efforts to become fitter, faster or stronger. Likewise in business: do the right thing, not the easiest; make the hard choices not the simple ones. As the famous saying goes, 'Pain is weakness leaving the body.' So get uncomfortable and set yourself up for success.

Saying you're going to make it home via the hard road is one thing. Actually seeing it through is an altogether different story and, truly, one of the only ways to achieve your goals is to have a *reason* for moving from A to B in the first place. One of the things I've always kept in mind during a period of suffering is the end result, whether that be a life in the military elite, a chance to see my friends and family again after a period of sustained and bloody service, or an exciting life in a challenging new career. Those carrots, left dangling at the end of a stick, have led me through some sticky situations where I've pushed myself through to the end by imagining a future win, or a moment of happiness. Really, with discipline installed, the only question I've had to ask myself is this: *Mate, how much do you want it?*

This is the spirit that drives an individual through Selection. I doubt there's anyone on earth who's stepped into that challenge believing it to be easy, or thinking, 'Do you know what? I'm not that bothered; I'm just going to turn up and I'm just going to crack it, because I'm fit and I'm capable.' I learned that the secret sauce in passing Selection successfully isn't talent or brains. It's relentless effort and a good attitude. Of course, skill and power are essential ingredients, but without desire and a team ethic, failure is inevitable. Once that moment eventually arrives, when a student has had their emotional armour stripped away, and they're strung out, alone in the cold and the dark with nothing more than their thoughts for company, only a clear purpose or a visualized reward at the end will carry them through.

When I was working in the military my purposes were fairly easy to comprehend. As a Royal Marine I wanted to understand where my limitations ended and so I pushed myself towards them whenever I could. The results of this mindset were incredibly satisfying: I was awarded the Physical Training medal for being the fittest guy in the troop. I was also presented with the King's Badge, a medal given to the best recruit overall to finish basic training, because I was generally the fastest on the Commando trials and across the Bottom Field assault course. Even though I led the pack a lot of the time, I rarely slowed down for anything.

This was most evident during a 'mud run' that was conducted

at the estuary in Exmouth. As the name suggests this was a horrible event and it was often conducted when the troop had fucked up on a training exercise, though we suspected that the senior commanders simply enjoyed thrashing us for their own personal amusement. The exercise was a grind: mud sucked at my ankles and shins as I sprinted and I was forced to perform Commando crawls, baby crawls and fireman's carries through the heavy sludge. During my first mud run, some lads around me puked up and passed out. Physically we were being put to the flame, but I didn't give a shit and I kept going until I was the last man standing. In my head the test was going to finish at any minute and I wanted to move until the very end. What I hadn't known was that the test only ended once the last man had collapsed. Eventually I located my breaking point. I face-planted into the mud after nearly blacking out, but I had pushed myself to the max.

Having served in the Marines for a few years, my motivations changed. I was bored, the wind had gone out of my sails, and having seen the military elite in action while on a tour of duty, my eyes were opened to another world. 'Oh, fucking hell,' I thought, 'the Royal Marines were the best of the best in my head, but I now know there's another level.' Don't get me wrong: the Marines are an incredible group; serving with them was a noble act and a fine career. It's just that simply knowing there was something beyond that expert troop meant there was another target to strive for. *And the hard road would get me there.*

Passing Selection became an obsession and there was no way I wanted to give up on it, though I was pushed to my absolute limits. There were times when I felt physically thrashed, while operating in some of the harshest conditions a commando could possibly face, but I kept a single thought in my head: *I don't want to go back to the Marines. I want to scrap with the very best.* It kept me going whenever my legs felt like they wanted to buckle, or I was having to fireman's carry a teammate up a steep and slippery hill.

Whatever your motivation is – and it could be familial security, financial freedom, creative satisfaction, autonomy, a bunch of trophies in the psychological cabinet – remember this: achieving a goal is supposed to be tough, so take pleasure in the grind because the only way you can get to where you want to be is through working relentlessly. It's also worth noting that your circumstances won't count for anything. It might be that you've been pushed into a hard spot by misfortune. You might have been brought up in tough conditions, or you may have experienced a financial or personal disaster later on in life. On the other side of that, you might be one of the lucky 1 per centers born with a silver spoon in your mouth. Either way, you're the author of your own story. There are different narratives to follow and plot twists to live. You can either make it a classic or a bargain bin throwaway, but the epic tale doesn't happen without discomfort.

More than anything, I've learned that failure is an emotional nightmare. But rather than avoiding it, I've faced up to the fear of defeat and used it to push me on. I think it's helped that I was given an important lesson from a very early age: life isn't fair. My mum's passing proved that. Then, when a promising football career was cut short, that truth was only underlined further. It also made me appreciate that I had responsibilities to other people. After my bike crash I knew I'd fucked up. But I also understood that I'd let down some people who had put their time, effort and faith into my development. That really stung, though it created a massive shift in attitude. I took the failures as lessons. 'This is on me,' I thought. 'I need to crack on here.' By the time I'd made it to Selection, I'd learned to push myself to the limit.

What I'm saying is that the next steps are now upon you. The chapters within *The Hard Road Will Take You Home* have delivered the tools needed to achieve success and, by using them, maybe a series of results you once considered beyond your reach. Ultimately, though, I can't force you down the hard road. *Only you can do that*. What I can tell you is that the very first footfall will land once you've defined the one thing that means the most to you. Something that you're passionate about, such as a cause or a lifestyle that will make you *want* to push yourself to the absolute limit. So invest in your relationships, your business, your training, your challenges and your education, and tread the hard road, because avoiding pain is the fast track to disappointment. And there's really no valour in that.

Endpapers:
Photography Credits

Image 1: Myself & Foxy taking the recruits through capsize drills on *SAS WDW*, 2020

Image 2: Myself, Mark Ormrod MBE & Louis at ThruDark HQ, 2021

Image 3: Louis Tinsley, Sam Sheriff & myself beginning our jiu-jitsu journey, 2021 (Matt Hardy)

Image 4: Myself, Steve Clark & Louis Tinsley, 2021 (Matt Hardy)

Image 5: Myself, Foxy, Dylan Hartley, Dave Morton and Louis on top of the iconic Pen Y Fan, 2021 (Matt Hardy)

Image 6: Me and my wife Ruby after tying the knot, 2021 (Emma Hurley)

Image 7: Myself, Ruby, Lucas (9), Albie (4) & Hughie (6 months), 2021 (Emma Hurley)

Image 8: Abseiling into the Mer De Glace, France, during a ThruDark product testing trip, 2019 (Matt Hardy)

Image 9: Nimsdai Purja & myself catching a ride from Namche Bazaar, 2021 (Hamish Frost)

Image 10: Climbing Ama Dablam between camp 1 and 2, 2021 (Hamish Frost)

Image 11: My wedding speech addressing my dear grandparents, 2021 (Emma Hurley)

Image 12: Love many, trust few, always paddle your own canoe. Myself & Louis, 2018

Image 13: Testing our ThruDark Force Range in the Faroe Islands, 2023 (Niklas Soderlund)

Image 14: Receiving my blue belt promotion from my instructor Nathan Johnstone, 2022 (Matt Hardy)

Image 15: Louis & myself at the Bremont Mayfair store for the ThruDark launch event, 2018 (Greg Williams)

Image 16: Product testing the new ThruDark snow range in France, 2022 (Niklas Soderlund)

Image 17: Ama Dablam summit 6,812m, 2021 (Hamish Frost)

Image 18: Remembrance Day with Albie, 2019

Image 19: Receiving my CGC at Windsor Castle from HRH Queen Elizabeth II, 2014

Image 20: *SAS Who Dares Wins* with fellow DS Ant Middleton, Jason Fox, Melvyn Downes & Billy Billingham, 2020

ACKNOWLEDGEMENTS

The Hard Road Will Take You Home, and the feelings and words captured within it, have been a manifestation of hours of hard work behind the scenes between myself and my good friend Matt Allen, to whom I owe a debt of gratitude for his patience and perseverance. Without him, this book would have been nothing more than a few incoherent scribbles from myself about my eventful life to date. Thank you Matt!

The book draws on my personal experiences from my military past, life hardships and lessons learned along the way. ThruDark, it's fair to say, thus far has been a dream only made possible by the people currently within its organization. Leaving the military elite was one of my most difficult decisions to date, however, having our good friend and founding investor Steve Clark on hand to help guide the way eased this burden. To my brother Louis Tinsley, I am blessed to have you as a friend and business cofounder – from door kickers to fabric pullers, who would have thought? I couldn't have asked for a better man to have by my side in business, and in life.

Seeing and hearing my own experiences would not have been made possible without the amazing support from the whole publishing team at Allen & Unwin (Atlantic Books). Ed Faulkner in particular shared my vision early on and was instrumental in getting this book to print. His small yet dynamic team punch big and were always on hand to offer support and guidance throughout. Team work makes the dream work.

I'd also like to take this opportunity to thank my very dear friend, gifted writer and voice of reason, Chips Hardy. Always in the shadows, forever a calming voice of reason, integrity and knowledge. Thank you Chips!

Thank you to my friends and contacts who also contributed and added incredible value to the audio chapters, some absolute gold and knowledge bombs to be found!

To my family, my grandparents, who selflessly raised me, and instilled my core values. To my brother Andrew, for having my back in our darkest hours and giving me somebody to look up to.

Lucas, Albie & Hughie, my boys. The apple doesn't fall far from the tree. I'm incredibly proud of you all and hope this book inspires you to be the very best versions of yourselves. And finally, to my incredible wife Ruby, thank you for your constantly unwavering support, my beacon of light on the shore…